MW00985107

Praying with the Prophets

Other titles in the Praying with the Bible Series
by Eugene H. Peterson:

Praying with Jesus
Praying with the Psalms
Praying with the Early Christians
Praying with Moses
Praying with Paul

Other titles by Eugene H. Peterson:

Answering God
Reversed Thunder
The Message

PRAYING
WITH THE PROPHETS

A Year of Daily Prayers
and Reflections
on the Words and Actions
of the Prophets

EUGENE H. PETERSON

HarperSanFrancisco
An Imprint of HarperCollins*Publishers*

FIRST EDITION

Library of Congress Cataloging-in-Publication Data
Peterson, Eugene H.
    Praying with the prophets : a year of daily prayers and
  reflections on the words and actions of the prophets /
  Eugene H. Peterson.
      p.   cm.
    ISBN: 0-06-066431-2 (pbk.)
    1. Prophets—Prayer-books and devotions—English.
  2. Bible.   O.T.   Prophets—Devotional literature.
  3. Devotional calendars.   I. Title.
  BS1198.P47   1995   95-9267
  242'.2—dc20   CIP

95 96 97 98 99 ❖ BANWI 10 9 8 7 6 5 4 3 2

For
Elvira and Neville Jacobs
persevering in the prophetic life

Introduction

PRAYER IS the deepest, quite the most profound, activity that any of us—child, man, woman—is capable of. Nothing we do, think, say, or feel is more authentically itself than when it is prayed.

Two pillar truths support this: one, God is the defining reality of all that is, including us; two, God is personally present to us in all that we are and do. This is what Christians and Jews have always believed. It follows that when we pray, receiving God's personal presence and responding in kind, we are most in touch with reality—the Real World, the God World—and most ourselves, our true Image-of-God selves.

But this is not an understanding of prayer current in our culture. The modern world, at least when it gets down to what it thinks of as serious business, is suspicious of prayer. Sometimes it is downright hostile. Much of this suspicion derives from the "masters of suspicion" of the last hundred or so years who have treated prayer variously as a narcotic that dulls our sensibilities, incapacitating us for dealing with the hard task of living (Marx); as wishful fantasy, a childish escape into a dreamland where we never have to grow up and take on the demanding responsibilities of adulthood (Freud); and as a sieve into which we pour our powerful energies of will only to have them dissipated uselessl⸱ in the dirt (Nietzsche). Whether as narcotic, fantasy, or sieve, these are not images designed to bolster confidence in prayer.

If these images are accurate, the sooner prayer is discredited the better. Becoming and being human is an exacting enterprise—we cannot afford, nor should we tolerate, anything that dulls or distracts or dilutes our attention. But if the images are not accurate—worse, if they are just plain wrongheaded—then we will have been robbed of a way of being in which multimillions of men and women have found, and continue to find, their lives sharpened, targeted, and concentrated in such ways that they become more themselves, more human, not less.

At the same time, it is easy to find instances in our own lives or the lives of others when something called prayer has been used as a pious cover for living badly. Insofar as the masters of suspicion alert us to the possibility and prevalence of "unprayer," they do us a service. For not all prayer is prayer. Counterfeits abound.

But finding instances of the genuine article is even easier than detecting and exposing the false. Christians usually start with the Bible, learning to pray by praying along with those who have done it right. By praying our scriptures, not just gleaning information from them, or searching for inspiration in them, we acquire a taste for the real thing: prayer in which we become more ourselves, more alive to God, and more responsible to the world and community around us.

On the historical horizon, conspicuous among those whose prayers have pulled them out of the huddle of life-avoiding pieties and into the thick of life-affirming social and community responsibilities are the Hebrew prophets. Praying, they acquired stature and energy to deal with great issues of justice and peace, mercy and grace, salvation and judgment, politics and economics. If we pray in their company, we will not likely misconstrue prayer as withdrawal, as an escapist or private enterprise. Praying with the prophets is a primary way by which we fortify our prayers against the anemia and dilettantism of "unprayer."

Emerson's phrase "artful thunder" has long attached itself in my mind to the Hebrew prophets. Thunder is attention-getting. The rumble and crash of thunder forces us into an awareness of Weather, which we hardly notice on calm and sunny days. All the conditions for thunder, though always present, are usually unnoticed—moisture, wind currents, barometric pressure, temperature, electrical charges—but when the proportions and combinations of the elements are just right, there is thunder. We notice. Prophets constitute such moments. The taken-for-granted elements of life that for our ease and convenience we keep in separate categories—God and the soul, righteousness and injustice, politics and war, poverty and exploitation, public and private—come together in the prophet in a thunderclap. We run for cover, but there is no cover. We are caught, exposed, in the Weather, God's Weather—all of life.

But the prophets are not just thunderclaps, they are "*artful* thunder." They not only command our awareness, bringing us to attention before God's demanding presence; they artfully draw us into intricacies of spirit and complexities of society. Under the shaping influence of the exquisite beauties and true harmonies of God's Word, its sounds and rhythms and metaphors, our souls acquire the precision of a dancer, the energy of an athlete.

In praying the artful thunder of the prophets, we are kept in continuous company not only with God, but in God's love for the lost, passion for the poor, fierce judgments against evil, tender care for the homeless and outcasts—frontline participants in God's work of making a new heaven and a new earth.

I have selected five prophets for this year of praying: Jeremiah, Daniel, Hosea, Amos, and Micah. The five represent a wide range in both time and tone, so that as we pray with them we can, if we will, acquire facility of soul for living boldly and obediently in this world that Jesus so much loves and died to save.

It would greatly please me if this book, designed to fit into purse or pocket so that it is readily available for use in the unscheduled, in-between moments of the day, would also be used to gather friends together, joining personal prayers to public concern, as the prophets teach us to do.

Praying with the Prophets

JANUARY 1

"The Words of Jeremiah"

Read Jeremiah 1:1–3

The words of Jeremiah son of Hilkiah, of
the priests who were in Anathoth in the
land of Benjamin, to whom the word of
the Lord came in the days of King Josiah
son of Amon of Judah, in the thirteenth
year of his reign.

Jeremiah 1:1–2

Jeremiah's forty years of ministry spanned prosperity and devastation. He began by preaching the
recovery of righteousness; he concluded by living
through the unleashing of judgment. His preaching touched all the heights and depths that human
beings experience before God.

What do you know about the times of Jeremiah?

PRAYER: God, take these passionate, prophetic
words of your servant Jeremiah and use them to
make my faith unwavering, my courage and my
hope unflinching. Use them to guide me through
prosperity and to preserve me in affliction. For
Jesus' sake. Amen.

"Before You Were Born"
Read Jeremiah 1:4–5

"Before I formed you in the womb
I knew you, and before you were
born I consecrated you; I appointed
you a prophet to the nations."

Jeremiah 1:5

Before we are, God is. His word provides the gracious conditions and defines the glorious destiny of persons set apart for God. God is always previous to us, anticipating our very existence by calling us to live in his love as participants in his salvation of us.

What is God's destiny for you?

PRAYER: "I find, I walk, I love, but oh the whole of love is but my answer, Lord, to thee! For thou wert long beforehand with my soul; always thou lovedst me" (*The Pilgrim Hymnal*). Amen.

"I Am Only a Boy"
Read Jeremiah 1:6–8

Then I said, "Ah, Lord God! Truly I do not
know how to speak, for I am only a
boy."

Jeremiah 1:6

Jeremiah excused himself on the grounds of his inexperience. It was a plausible excuse, but an excuse all the same, and disallowed by his Lord. God does not choose us because we are qualified; he chooses us in order to qualify us for what he wants us to do.

What excuses have you used to try to avoid doing God's will?

PRAYER: Lord, I'm so used to trying to get out of things because I feel inadequate that it is going to be hard to try to get into things on the simple grounds that you have commanded them. But by your grace I will live in response to your call and not in reaction to my feelings. Amen.

"Today I Appoint You"

Read Jeremiah 1:9–10

"See, today I appoint you over nations and
over kingdoms, to pluck up and to pull
down, to destroy and to overthrow, to
build and to plant."

Jeremiah 1:10

Jeremiah is not a politician ambitious to make the
nation strong; he is not an aspiring reformer hoping to make the people good: he is a commanded
prophet who will speak to the people words of
God that will free them from the growths and
structures of sin ("pluck up and pull down") and
guide them into constructive and fruitful lives of
faith ("build and plant").

What does "prophet" mean?

PRAYER: What is my work, dear God? What do
you want me to do? Call and command me. Put
your words into my mouth today so that as I speak
I will build in your name and plant by your grace,
through Jesus Christ. Amen.

"I Am Watching"

Read Jeremiah 1:11–12

Then the Lord said to me, "You have seen
well, for I am watching over my word
to perform it."

Jeremiah 1:12

An almond tree blossomed before it put forth
leaves, an early sign of spring, while the land was
yet chill from winter. Also, the name "almond
tree" in Hebrew is "watch." God uses both the
sight and the sound of the "watch tree" to reassure Jeremiah that he is watching over his word.

How would this reassure Jeremiah?

PRAYER: God, I have uncertainties and doubts about
so many things. Use the visible and sure promises
that blossom in trees and hills to remind me of the
invisible and sure promises that blossom in a bare
land and bring the fruit of salvation. Amen.

"I Am Calling"
Read Jeremiah 1:13–17

For now I am calling all the tribes of the
  kingdoms of the north, says the Lord;
  and they shall come and all of them shall
  set their thrones at the entrance of the
  gates of Jerusalem, against all its
  surrounding walls and against all the
  cities of Judah.

Jeremiah 1:15

Nations to the north of Judah were already boiling with war plans. But that seething turbulence on the horizon was not, as it might seem, a wild, uncontrollable evil, but a carefully commanded judgment—with God as the commander.

How would this reassure Jeremiah?

PRAYER: Almighty Lord, I forget that the newspapers are footnotes to your word, not the other way around. Show me how to interpret the signs of the times by your word, and so find hope and courage where others in despair see only chaos. *Amen.*

JANUARY 7

"I Am with You"
Read Jeremiah 1:18–19

They will fight against you; but they shall
not prevail against you, for I am with
you, says the Lord, to deliver you.

Jeremiah 1:19

God gave his prophet three images of strength by
which to understand the reality of his vocation. In
the years that followed, Jeremiah often felt weak;
in fact, he always was strong. His emotions often
failed him; his faith always held fast. God's word
proved true.

What are the three images?

PRAYER: I accept your word to Jeremiah as your
promise to me, Almighty God. I will believe what
you say you are making me, rather than what others
say about me or what I feel about myself. In
Jesus' name. Amen.

"The Devotion of Your Youth"

Read Jeremiah 2:1–3

Go and proclaim in the hearing of Jerusalem, Thus says the Lord: I remember
the devotion of your youth, your love
as a bride, how you followed me in the
wilderness, in a land not sown.

Jeremiah 2:2

Jeremiah's first sermon recalls those early years in
the wilderness when, before the distractions of society and agriculture, the people themselves were
the bride and the harvest of God. In those simpler
days, the great reality of their lives was God's love
for them, God's work in them.

What good things do you remember of the wilderness years?

PRAYER: Why do I forget so quickly, abandon so
readily, my beginnings in your love, O Christ?
When I try to improve my life by adding things to
it, show me instead how to deepen it by returning
to the basics of your love and blessing. *Amen.*

"What Wrong?"

Read Jeremiah 2:4–8

Hear the word of the Lord, O house of
Jacob, and all the families of the house
of Israel. Thus says the Lord: What
wrong did your ancestors find in me
that they went far from me and went
after worthless things, and became
worthless themselves?

Jeremiah 2:4–5

The people are put to an examination. The results
show that the present disorder is a result of long-
standing and willful negligence—the failure of
parents and priests to ask the simple, obvious
question, "Where is the Lord?" and then to walk
in the path that led to him.

What was the result of the negligence?

PRAYER: Holy and eternal Father, you are at the
center of all life. I will arrange all my thoughts
and my ways in an act of adoration to you. I will
bow down and worship, and I will get up and follow, in praise and in faith. *Amen.*

JANUARY 10

"Cracked Cisterns"

Read Jeremiah 2:9–13

> For my people have committed two evils:
> they have forsaken me, the fountain of
> living water, and dug out cisterns for
> themselves, cracked cisterns that can
> hold no water.
>
> Jeremiah 2:13

An artesian well, spouting a continuous flow of fresh water, is contrasted with a broken cistern, incapable of holding the precious rainwater that fell into it. Is it conceivable that anyone would abandon the flowing fountain for the cracked and leaky cistern? Yet these people had forsaken the living God and taken up with wooden-headed gods.

Where is Cyprus? Where is Kedar?

PRAYER: Give me, all-wise God, the quick-eyed ability to see the stupidity and scandal of making a religion out of things and superstitions. And deepen my hunger and thirst for a righteousness that can be satisfied only at the table you set before me. *Amen.*

"Is Israel a Slave?"

Read Jeremiah 2:14–19

> Is Israel a slave? Is he a homeborn servant?
>   Why then has he become plunder?
>
> Jeremiah 2:14

Set free from all sin-slavery, Israel was free to follow God and live in praise to his glory. Every time she forsook that heritage she paid for it in new forms of bondage. The only path to freedom—how much trial-and-error experimentation does it take to convince us of this?—is the path to God.

Note the two places where the verb "forsake" is used.

PRAYER: Lord Jesus Christ, I thank you for the freedom in which you have set me free. Help me to stand fast in it and never again submit to any yoke of slavery. Amen.

"On Every High Hill"

Read Jeremiah 2:20–25

> For long ago you broke your yoke and
> burst your bonds, and you said, "I will
> not serve!" On every high hill and under
> every green tree you sprawled and played
> the whore.

Jeremiah 2:20

Israel had a long history of unfaithfulness. Any attractively packaged religious promise was enough
to distract her from her commitment to her Lord;
every new religious fad was taken up and tried in
a burst of short-lived enthusiasm. For centuries it
had been one religious "lover" after another.

What do you know about Baal worship?

PRAYER: God Almighty, keep me faithful to your
faithfulness: arrest me when I wander from the
path of your righteousness; stop me when I turn
back to old slave habits; keep me steadily true to
your love in Jesus Christ. *Amen.*

"Where Are Your Gods?"

Read Jeremiah 2:26–32

> But where are your gods that you made
> for yourself? Let them come, if they can
> save you, in your time of trouble; for you
> have as many gods as you have towns,
> O Judah.

Jeremiah 2:28

The people were religious enough: they called a tree "father" and they named the stone "mother." They had a god for every occasion, a god to fit every mood. But it was a stupid religion. How was it possible for people to forget a living relationship with a loving God and immerse themselves in such nonsense? Yet it happened. And it still happens.

What "gods" are you aware of today?

PRAYER: Holy Father, you have revealed yourself awesomely in love, in Christ. And I have experienced that love. Keep me faithful to the best you have given me as I make my way through the superstitious substitutes and cheap imitations that promise religious benefits and make no demands. They are so shoddy! Defend me against them and keep me faithful to your upward call in Christ Jesus. *Amen.*

"How Lightly You Gad About"
Read Jeremiah 2:33–37

How lightly you gad about, changing
your ways! You shall be put to shame
by Egypt as you were put to shame by
Assyria.

Jeremiah 2:36

Israel is like a giddy, flirtatious girl, flitting from
one relationship to another, careless of all responsibilities, and naively disavowing any wrongdoing. But no people can live like this and get away
with it. God will not permit the people he loves
and the people he created for glory to live in such
silliness and emptiness.

Compare the images in verses 26 and 36.

PRAYER: Lord, help me to live according to your
grand design in Jesus. You have higher goals for
me than I have for myself: you see so much more
meaning for me than I have discerned on my
own. Use your judgments to separate me from
frivolous pursuits and unworthy ambitions, and
lead me in your more excellent way. Amen.

"You Have Polluted the Land"

Read Jeremiah 3:1–5

Look up to the bare heights, and see!
    Where have you not been lain with?
    By the waysides you have sat waiting for
    lovers, like a nomad in the wilderness.
    You have polluted the land with your
    whoring and wickedness.

Jeremiah 3:2

Moral pollution works much the same way as environmental pollution. The waste product of careless living that is indifferent to consequences insidiously works itself into the soil of thought and streams of language and causes damage to generations yet unborn.

What kind of moral pollution is taking place today?

PRAYER: The danger, Lord, when I realize the extent of moral pollution in the land, is that I become overwhelmed and paralyzed into inaction. Protect me from despair and show me what I can say and do today that will be signs of the new heaven and earth that you are making. *Amen.*

"Only in Pretense"

Read Jeremiah 3:6–10

> Yet for all this her false sister Judah did not
> return to me with her whole heart, but
> only in pretense, says the Lord.
>
> Jeremiah 3:10

Israel, the northern part of the kingdom, had broken away from loyal worship and service to her Lord a hundred years or so earlier than Judah in the south. There was judgment in the form of invasion and exile. Warned by those consequences, Judah underwent a superficial reformation. But it was all pretense—in actual practice she continued as faithless as her northern sister.

What do you know about Israel's judgment?

PRAYER: Eternal God, make the inside and outside of my life the same. Make my words honest expressions of my thoughts, my actions true expressions of my decisions, and everything—word, thought, and deed—subject to your scrutiny and judgment. *Amen.*

JANUARY 17

"Return, Faithless Israel"

Read Jeremiah 3:11–14

Go, and proclaim these words toward the
north, and say: Return, faithless Israel,
says the Lord. I will not look on you in
anger, for I am merciful, says the Lord;
I will not be angry forever.

Jeremiah 3:12

If we stay away from God because we are afraid of
his anger, we are making a great mistake. His atti-
tude to us—in our rebellion, in our faithlessness,
in our disobedience—is merciful. He invites us to
return and waits for us in mercy.

Are you afraid of God?

PRAYER: "God, be merciful to me, on thy grace I
rest my plea; plenteous in compassion thou, blot
out my transgressions now; wash me, make me
pure within, cleanse, oh cleanse me from my sin"
(*The Psalter*, 1912). *Amen.*

"Shepherds After My Own Heart"
Read Jeremiah 3:15–20

I will give you shepherds after my
own heart, who will feed you with
knowledge and understanding.

Jeremiah 3:15

Our ideas of what we want for ourselves and God's
plans for our salvation are at cross-purposes. All
the time we are wandering and rebelling, God is
developing strategies of salvation whereby we will
finally realize his bounty and peace.

Compare this with John 10:11–18.

PRAYER: Implant in me, O God, a deep desire for
realities that you are preparing me to possess—
your knowledge, your presence, your peace, your
heritage—so that I can live expectantly, in the right
direction. *Amen.*

JANUARY 19

"Truly the Hills Are a Delusion"
Read Jeremiah 3:21–24

Truly the hills are a delusion, the orgies
on the mountains. Truly in the Lord
our God is the salvation of Israel.

Jeremiah 3:23

The "hills" and the "mountains" were where Baal
worship flourished. Israel had squandered the
strength of her youth in chasing after the illusions
of pleasure fulfillment promised there. Now the
ardent, prophetic pleading is answered by a devout repentance.

Compare this with Psalm 121.

PRAYER: God, give me eyes to see through the false
promises made by the world around me; give me
ears to hear your word spoken for my salvation. In
the name of Jesus Christ, my Lord and Savior. *Amen.*

JANUARY 20

"Break Up Your Fallow Ground"
Read Jeremiah 4:1–4

For thus says the Lord to the people of
Judah and to the inhabitants of Jerusalem: Break up your fallow ground,
and do not sow among thorns.

Jeremiah 4:3

Indifference, hypocrisy, superstition, idolatry—
these form a tough crust or skin that makes us in-
sensitive and unreceptive to the word that God
speaks to us in salvation. Plowing and circumcis-
ing are metaphors for a repentance that prepares
the soil/flesh of our hearts to receive what God
has for us.

Compare this with Mark 4:3–9.

PRAYER: So many things get between you and me,
O God—pious habits, compulsive routines, un-
hallowed fantasies, and cherished illusions. Break
through them all and implant your word that will
bring forth a good harvest in my life, to your glory.
Amen.

"Prophets Astounded"

Read Jeremiah 4:5–10

On that day, says the Lord, courage shall
  fail the king and the officials; the priests
  shall be appalled and the prophets
  astounded.

Jeremiah 4:9

Many, and Jeremiah apparently among them, had
supposed that God's promised blessing was a guar-
antee against foreign invasion. But God's blessing—"it shall be well with you"—does not ex-
clude judgment; rather, it uses judgment to bring
about a final salvation.

Why is judgment so difficult to understand?

PRAYER: I try, Lord, to eliminate the difficult and to
avoid the unpleasant. I don't want to think about
it, and I don't want to experience it. Still, you face
me with it. Use it to make me whole, disciplining
and sanctifying me so that all will be well. *Amen.*

"Your Ways and Your Doings"
Read Jeremiah 4:11–18

Your ways and your doings have brought
 this upon you. This is your doom; how
 bitter it is! It has reached your very
 heart.

Jeremiah 4:18

One of Jeremiah's prophetic assignments was to develop a sense of responsibility among the people so that they would be deeply aware that all they did and said was moral—that it made a difference and had consequences. There are no neutral acts, no unimportant words.

How many images of judgment are there in these verses?

PRAYER: Use the great drama of judgment, Almighty God, to illuminate the significance of everything I do today, so that all my ways and my doings will be aspects of goodness by which you can will yourself through me. *Amen.*

JANUARY 23

"Skilled in Doing Evil"

Read Jeremiah 4:19–22

> For my people are foolish, they do not
> know me; they are stupid children, they
> have no understanding. They are skilled
> in doing evil, but do not know how to
> do good.
>
> Jeremiah 4:22

Jeremiah's sympathy for the people is countered
by God's unsentimental compassion. For a people
who have spent their lives developing skills for
getting their own way and are therefore absolutely ignorant of God's way, the cataclysm of
war is the only way to get their attention so that
they can be trained in righteousness.

What skills for doing good do you want to develop?

PRAYER: "Teach us to love the true, The beautiful
and pure, And let us not for one short hour An
evil thought endure. But give us grace to stand
Decided, brave and strong, The lovers of all holy
things, The foes of all things wrong" (Walter J.
Mathams, "Now in the Days of Youth," *The Hymnbook*, 469). *Amen.*

"Waste and Void"

Read Jeremiah 4:23–28

> I looked on the earth, and lo, it was waste
> and void; and to the heavens, and they
> had no light.
>
> Jeremiah 4:23

Here is a reversal of creation—an "uncreation." By using the language of Genesis, the prophet at one and the same time communicates the immensity of the judgment and the assurance of salvation, for it is precisely out of "waste and void" that God creates new life.

Read Genesis 1:1–3.

PRAYER: Speak your Genesis words over the waste and void of my life, Creator Christ, and bring forth light and singing and color and movement—a life lived to your glory in praise. *Amen.*

"In Vain You Beautify Yourself"

Read Jeremiah 4:29–31

And you, O desolate one, what do you
  mean that you dress in crimson, that
  you deck yourself with ornaments of
  gold, that you enlarge your eyes with
  paint? In vain you beautify yourself.
  Your lovers despise you; they seek your
  life.

Jeremiah 4:30

Do these people think that by using cosmetics
they can change their destiny? It is they themselves who need to be changed. And judgment
will do it. It will be calamitous and it will be
painful—it will seem like the end of everything—
but it will be the beginning of their salvation.

Compare this with Jesus' words in Matthew
23:27–28.

PRAYER: You force me, O Christ, to face the deepest truths about myself, the truth of my sin and
the truth of your salvation, and find myself face-
to-face with a Redeemer to whom I now submit
myself in awe and adoration. *Amen.*

"See If You Can Find"

Read Jeremiah 5:1–3

Run to and fro through the streets of
   Jerusalem, look around and take note!
   Search its squares and see if you can find
   one person who acts justly and seeks
   truth—so that I may pardon Jerusalem.

Jeremiah 5:1

The ancient Greeks told a similar story: Old
Diogenes went through the streets and alleys of
Athens, day after day, carrying a lantern in search
of an honest man. He never found one. Jeremiah
was likewise unsuccessful.

What truthful, honest people do you know?

PRAYER: "Investigate my life, O God, find out everything about me; Cross-examine and test me, get a
clear picture of what I'm about; See for yourself
whether I've done anything wrong—then guide
me on the road to eternal life" (Psalm 139:23–24).
Amen.

"All Alike Had Broken the Yoke"
Read Jeremiah 5:4–9

"Let me go to the rich and speak to them;
  surely they know the way of the Lord,
  the law of their God." But they all alike
  had broken the yoke, they had burst the
  bonds.

Jeremiah 5:5

Jeremiah discovers that sin knows no class lines: the intelligent are no less rebellious than the stupid, the literate than the illiterate, the rich than the poor, the powerful than the weak.

Do you think that other people are more liable to sin than you?

PRAYER: Your searching word, O God, discovers all my hiding places. When I try to hide behind my knowledge, or my possessions, or my reputation, or even my good intentions, your word finds me out. Since hiding doesn't work, save me and bless me, for Jesus' sake. *Amen.*

"But Do Not Make a Full End"
Read Jeremiah 5:10–17

Go up through her vine-rows and destroy,
  but do not make a full end; strip away
  her branches, for they are not the Lord's.
                                    Jeremiah 5:10

Terrible as the impending judgment will be, it will not mean the annihilation of the people. The punishing invasion by the "ancient nation" (Babylonia) will have a purging effect on the people and will make them into disciplined pilgrims.

Compare this with John 15:1–2.

PRAYER: Merciful and gracious Christ, help me to accept the chastening of your judgment as the pruning of the vinedresser. Strip from my life all that does not grow from your planting, so that I may bear the good fruit of righteousness. *Amen.*

JANUARY 29

"Strangers in a Land"
Read Jeremiah 5:18–19

And when your people say, "Why has the
Lord our God done all these things to
us?" you shall say to them, "As you have
forsaken me and served foreign gods in
your land, so you shall serve strangers
in a land that is not yours."

Jeremiah 5:19

In a few years the people of Israel would be taken
six hundred miles into exile in Babylon, a strange
land. It was a terrible judgment, but it had won-
derful consequences, for there they learned to
value their unique heritage, to worship, and to be
loyal to their Lord.

Read Psalm 137.

PRAYER: Father in heaven, never turn away from
me, but always confront me with your will. When
I face your judgments, I find, finally, mercy at the
center of them. For your faithfulness and mercy I
thank you. *Amen.*

JANUARY 30

"They Know No Limits"
Read Jeremiah 5:20–29

They have grown fat and sleek. They know
no limits in deeds of wickedness; they
do not judge with justice the cause of
the orphan, to make it prosper, and they
do not defend the rights of the needy.

Jeremiah 5:28

Oceans and lakes know and respect the boundaries set for them by God (v. 22). Why will not human beings do the same? But everywhere there are people who scorn and flout guidelines of justice and gratitude, compassion and generosity.

Compare this imagery with Romans 1:19–23.

PRAYER: Dear God, I want to live in harmony with what you have created in and around me, not at odds with it. I want to increase in wisdom and stature, in favor with God and humanity (Luke 2:52). Amen.

"Appalling and Horrible"

Read Jeremiah 5:30–31

An appalling and horrible thing has
   happened in the land: the prophets
   prophesy falsely, and the priests rule
   as the prophets direct; my people love
   to have it so, but what will you do
   when the end comes?

Jeremiah 5:30–31

Jeremiah can think of nothing worse: the prophets set aside for the awesome responsibility of
proclaiming God's truth tell lies; the priests commissioned to guide seekers after God into the way
of righteousness advise them with falsehoods.
And instead of being laughed at or thrown out,
they have become the darlings of the people.

   Is this going on in our land, do you think?

PRAYER: God, give me a desire for what is true, a
hunger for what is righteous, and a determination
to refuse all substitutes, no matter how attractively
presented. In the name of Jesus Christ, my Lord and
Savior. *Amen.*

"Blow the Trumpet in Tekoa"

Read Jeremiah 6:1–5

Flee for safety, O children of Benjamin,
from the midst of Jerusalem! Blow the
trumpet in Tekoa, and raise a signal on
Beth-haccherem; for evil looms out of
the north, and great destruction.

Jeremiah 6:1

Generations of sinful, disobedient, and faithless living result in a society that is sodden, apathetic, unaware. The sharp trumpet blasts of judgment are an attempt to wake us up to the fact that God is real and alive in our midst.

What has God used to wake you up?

PRAYER: God, I get so absorbed in my day-to-day routines that I lose all consciousness of your commanding word, all awareness of your holy will. When that happens, set off your judgment alarm so that I will be awake to what you are doing. *Amen.*

"She Keeps Fresh Her Wickedness"
Read Jeremiah 6:6–8

As a well keeps its water fresh, so she
keeps fresh her wickedness; violence
and destruction are heard within her;
sickness and wounds are ever before me.
Jeremiah 6:7

Jerusalem was designated the center for Israel's worship. All the people, from all parts of Israel, came to worship at the temple. There the sacrifices were renewed daily and the word of God was announced freshly. But, sadly, the city had become instead a center for wickedness. A zest for righteousness had given way to the latest in wickedness.

What are some of the "sickness and wounds" in our land?

PRAYER: Lord Jesus Christ, the world around me is untiring in its attempts to package faded and banal sins in eye-catching shapes and colors. But for all the attractive packaging, they are the same old "sickness and wounds." Let me not be tempted by them. Amen.

"Treated the Wound of My People Carelessly"
Read Jeremiah 6:9–15

They have treated the wound of my people
   carelessly, saying, "Peace, peace," when
   there is no peace.

Jeremiah 6:14

The wounds that sin has inflicted on society are
deep and dangerous. But if the wounds are covered over with decorative bandages, and everyone
is cheerfully complimentary of the nice bandages
and does nothing about the terrible wounds, will
healing take place? Not until the bandages are
ripped off and the wounds themselves are treated
by the Master Physician.

What are some sin-wounds in our society?

PRAYER: O God, help me to honestly face what is
wrong in my life and then to confess and be
healed. I do not want superficial cheeriness; I do
not want a facade of well-being. I want the peace
that passes understanding. *Amen.*

"Ask for the Ancient Paths"

Read Jeremiah 6:16–21

Thus says the Lord: Stand at the crossroads,
and look, and ask for the ancient paths,
where the good way lies; and walk in it,
and find rest for your souls. But they
said, "We will not walk in it."

Jeremiah 6:16

There are ancient paths, well trodden and clearly marked, that lead to goodness and to God. If we choose another way, or wander down another path, God calls out a warning. If we do not respond, he puts obstacles, stumbling blocks, in our way. He is tireless in his attempts to return us to a life of faith and righteousness.

What are the ancient paths?

PRAYER: Lord, when I am interrupted or frustrated or defeated, instead of angrily complaining, I will first ask if it might not be a warning from you to prevent me from pursuing a wrong way, or persisting in an unprofitable venture. Amen.

"Most Bitter Lamentation"
Read Jeremiah 6:22–26

O my poor people, put on sackcloth, and
    roll in ashes; make mourning as for
    an only child, most bitter lamentation:
    for suddenly the destroyer will come
    upon us.

Jeremiah 6:26

There is no negotiating with the word of judgment, and there is no escaping it. It must be met. But there are appropriate and inappropriate ways to meet it—inappropriately with denial or defiance; appropriately with lamentation and repentance, symbolized in sackcloth and ashes.

How do you express your penitence before God?

PRAYER: "Just as I am, and waiting not To rid my soul of one dark blot, To Thee, whose blood can cleanse each spot, O Lamb of God, I come, I come" (Charlotte Elliott, "Just as I Am, Without One Plea," *The Hymnbook*, 272). *Amen.*

"A Tester and a Refiner"
Read Jeremiah 6:27–30

I have made you a tester and a refiner
among my people so that you may
know and test their ways.

Jeremiah 6:27

The prophet's task was to test the metal of the people to see what they were made of. The test results showed only slag. In spite of the fierce fires of preached judgment to which they had been exposed, none of the impurities of their lives had been removed.

Compare a similar sermon in Isaiah 1:25.

PRAYER: God Almighty, as you face me with your searching, purifying word, do your refining work in me so that I may be made useful and valuable for exchanges of grace in the economy of your kingdom. Amen.

"These Deceptive Words"

Read Jeremiah 7:1–7

Do not trust in these deceptive words:
"This is the temple of the Lord, the
temple of the Lord, the temple of the
Lord."

Jeremiah 7:4

Jeremiah's famous "temple sermon": preaching from the steps of the temple, he denounces the people for absurdly thinking that by intoning a pious phrase ("This is the temple of the Lord") they will protect themselves from the consequences of their violent ways.

How many sins are listed?

PRAYER: Holy God, I want every word I speak in worship to be an honest expression of what I am living every day, so that worship becomes an offering up of my life to your glory, not a cover-up of my sin. *Amen.*

"Just What I Did to Shiloh"

Read Jeremiah 7:8–15

Therefore I will do to the house that is
called by my name, in which you trust,
and to the place that I gave to you and to
your ancestors, just what I did to Shiloh.

Jeremiah 7:14

If the people foolishly suppose that the mere presence of the temple is going to protect them from
judgment, all they have to do is walk twenty miles
north to Shiloh and look at the pile of rubble that
was once the shrine housing the Ark of the Covenant.

Compare Jesus' use of this passage in his temple sermon (Mark 11:15–19).

PRAYER: Lord God, help me to read the lessons of
history rightly and observe all the evidence carefully, so that I may profit from the mistakes of my
ancestors and not merely repeat their sins. Amen.

"Cakes for the Queen of Heaven"
Read Jeremiah 7:16–29

> The children gather wood, the fathers
> kindle fire, and the women knead
> dough, to make cakes for the queen
> of heaven; and they pour out drink
> offerings to other gods, to provoke
> me to anger.
>
> Jeremiah 7:18

Anyone walking through the streets of Jerusalem in Jeremiah's day would have been impressed with the sheer quantity and energy of the religious life. Everyone was involved in some kind of religious activity. And everyone was ignoring God.

Compare this with Psalm 50:12–18.

PRAYER: Continue to speak your searching, commanding, saving word to me, merciful God. Batter down the walls of indifference in my life. Penetrate the thick skin of my self-interest so that I may daily hear your gracious word and accept your saving love. Amen.

"They Will Bury in Topheth"
Read Jeremiah 7:30–34

Therefore, the days are surely coming,
   says the Lord, when it will no more be
   called Topheth, or the valley of the son
   of Hinnom, but the valley of Slaughter:
   for they will bury in Topheth until there
   is no more room.

Jeremiah 7:32

In the valley south of Jerusalem, an illicit place of worship, Topheth, had been set up. The place was thronged with fanatical religious thrill-seekers. God's judgment, says the prophet, will turn the popular and corrupt center of religious fervor into a vast graveyard filled with corpses.

Locate Topheth on a map of Jerusalem.

PRAYER: I pray today, Lord, for people who are misguided in their faith, tangled in corrupt superstitions, seeking life but only corrupting and destroying their souls. Reveal Christ to them so they may worship you, the true and living God. *Amen.*

"This Evil Family"

Read Jeremiah 8:1–3

> Death shall be preferred to life by all the
> remnant that remains of this evil family
> in all the places where I have driven
> them, says the Lord of hosts.
>
> *Jeremiah 8:3*

"My chosen people," carelessly abandoning the magnificent austerities of a rich salvation by faith and squandering themselves in the sordid idolatries of the prevalent paganism, have now become "this evil family." The worst is the corruption of the best. "Lilies that fester smell far worse than weeds" (Shakespeare).

Compare this with Ezekiel 37.

PRAYER: God, I forget who I am; I forget in whose image I was made; I forget the high calling you have set out for me; I forget that I was bought with a price. And then, in your word I see myself as in a mirror, and am shocked into remembrance of your love and your purposes yet to be completed in me in Christ Jesus. *Amen.*

"Perpetual Backsliding"
Read Jeremiah 8:4–7

> Why then has this people turned away in
> perpetual backsliding? They have held
> fast to deceit, they have refused to
> return.
>
> Jeremiah 8:5

Look at the migratory patterns of the birds, says the prophet. They leave but they always come back. They have an instinctual sense of return. How much more must a person know, deeply and instinctively, that there is a time for coming home to God.

How many illustrations of repentance are there here?

PRAYER: "Just as I am, Thou wilt receive, Wilt welcome, pardon, cleanse, relieve; Because Thy promise I believe, O Lamb of God, I come, I come!" (Charlotte Elliott, "Just as I Am, Without One Plea," *The Hymnbook*, 272). *Amen.*

"The False Pen of the Scribes"

Read Jeremiah 8:8–13

> How can you say, "We are wise, and the
> law of the Lord is with us," when, in
> fact, the false pen of the scribes has
> made it into a lie?

Jeremiah 8:8

As these people write with their lives what they read in the book of God's law, they distort it into a falsehood. Their actions and speech are a "false pen." There is no recognizable relation between what they read and what they live.

Compare this with the parallel in chapter 6, verses 9–15.

PRAYER: Thank you, Almighty God, for words of wisdom and truth written in scripture and incarnate in Christ. By your Holy Spirit transcribe the words accurately and surely into my speech and action today. *Amen.*

"My Heart Is Sick"
Read Jeremiah 8:14–20

My joy is gone, grief is upon me, my heart
   is sick.

Jeremiah 8:18

The people have refused to repent; judgment now
appears inevitable, and Jeremiah's heart breaks.
He longs desperately for the salvation of this people hardened in their sin. Jeremiah is plunged into
grief.

Compare this weeping with Matthew 23:37–39.

PRAYER: God of all comfort, give me such a spirit
of compassion that when I am faced with rejection and indifference I may respond with determined intercession, after the manner of Jeremiah
and, even more, of Christ. *Amen.*

"No Balm in Gilead?"
Read Jeremiah 8:21–22

Is there no balm in Gilead? Is there no
physician there? Why then has the
health of my poor people not been
restored?

Jeremiah 8:22

Balm was used medicinally in the ancient world.
But there is neither medicine nor physician that
can heal sin's wound. Only God can bring health
to the "sin-sick soul." For as long as the people
refuse him, they are going to be sick.

Where is Gilead?

PRAYER: So many, Lord, long for healing; so many
look for easy remedies to their ill-conceived lives
and their unhappy careers. But they look in the
wrong places and go to the wrong persons. How
long until they cease looking vainly in Gilead and
come to you, the Great Physician? *Amen.*

FEBRUARY 16

"My Eyes a Fountain of Tears"
Read Jeremiah 9:1–3

O that my head were a spring of water,
  and my eyes a fountain of tears, so that
  I might weep day and night for the slain
  of my poor people!

Jeremiah 9:1

Jeremiah's capacity for compassion was profound; his willingness to share sorrow was endless; his passion for salvation was determined. In spite of his longings to get away from the people because of their evil ways, he stuck with them because of God's love.

Whose life do you feel compassion for?

PRAYER: "A broken heart, a fount of tears, Ask, and they will not be denied; A broken heart love's cradle is: Jesus, our Lord, is crucified!" (Frederick W. Faber, "O Come and Mourn with Me Awhile," *The Hymnbook*, 192). *Amen.*

"Supplanters"

Read Jeremiah 9:4–9

Beware of your neighbors, and put no trust
    in any of your kin; for all your kin are
    supplanters, and every neighbor goes
    around like a slanderer.

Jeremiah 9:4

If people will not trust in God, they very soon
come to the point where they cannot trust one another. Human trust and respect can be sustained
and developed only from a center of faith and reverence before God. Jacob is the archsupplanter in
the biblical story, and there is a pun on his name
here—"every brother's as crafty as Jacob" (John
Bright).

    Compare a similar indictment in Hosea 12:2–3.

PRAYER: I bring the people I love and with whom
I work before you, dear God; only in your presence will we learn to trust and serve, to laugh and
play. Reveal yourself to us. Show us how in loving
you to love one another. *Amen.*

FEBRUARY 18

"A Lair of Jackals"
Read Jeremiah 9:10–16

I will make Jerusalem a heap of ruins, a lair
of jackals; and I will make the towns of
Judah a desolation, without inhabitant.
Jeremiah 9:11

Two passages are placed alongside each other, one
prophesying the devastation of Jerusalem if there
is no repentance (vv. 10–11), the other surveying
the ruins after the devastation has taken place (vv.
12–16). The before and after views emphasize the
message: stubborn disobedience will end up a
heap of ruins.

How would you apply this to our society?

PRAYER: Father in heaven, give me the good sense
and a heart of repentance to respond to your relentless love. The evidence is plain and cumulative
that a life lived in defiance of your will is doomed
and wasted. And I want to be saved and blessed.
Amen.

"Death Has Come up into Our Windows"
Read Jeremiah 9:17–22

"Death has come up into our windows,
    it has entered our palaces, to cut off the
    children from the streets and the young
    men from the squares."

Jeremiah 9:21

A rejection of God is at the same time an invitation to death. We should not be surprised, then, when death comes like a thief climbing through the window and robbing us of what is most valuable, or like a scythe prematurely cutting down children and youth before they are fully grown. The only alternative to the life God gives is death.

Compare verse 18 with verse 1.

PRAYER: Help me to see, dear God, the consequences of each choice I make—that it leads either to life with you or to death apart from you; and give me the courage and wisdom to choose life, in the name of him who conquered death Amen.

"Boast"

Read Jeremiah 9:23–26

Thus says the Lord: Do not let the wise
boast in their wisdom, do not let the
mighty boast in their might, do not let
the wealthy boast in their wealth.

Jeremiah 9:23

Any gift or ability separated from God who gave it
becomes a curse. There are blessings associated
with health and wealth and wisdom, but they are
nothing to be proud of, only grateful for. Glorious
living consists in understanding the living Lord
and responding to the way he lives in the world,
practicing steadfast love, justice, and righteousness.

Compare this with 1 Corinthians 1:26–31.

PRAYER: I glory in your way, glorious God, and
boast of your goodness. I praise your acts of justice and sing your words of mercy. "Join me in
spreading the news; together let's get the word
out" (Psalm 34:3). *Amen.*

"No Better Than Wood"
Read Jeremiah 10:1–10

They are both stupid and foolish; the
instruction given by idols is no better
than wood!

Jeremiah 10:8

The ways of worship in the nations surrounding
Israel were impressive, with their elaborately
carved and gaudily decorated idols around which
intricate rituals were conducted. In comparison,
all Israel had was an invisible word to listen to. But
for all their impressiveness, the idols were dumb;
and what is a god good for if he can't tell you
what you don't already know or make you into
something you cannot make yourself?

Are you impressed by idols?

PRAYER: Lord, I am too easily impressed by size
and noise and sensation; and I am too quickly distracted from silence and listening and adoring.
But "there is none like thee, O Lord." Return me
to the silence where I can be shaped by your living word. Amen.

"Put to Shame by Their Idols"

Read Jeremiah 10:11–16

Everyone is stupid and without knowledge;
   goldsmiths are all put to shame by their
   idols; for their images are false, and there
   is no breath in them.

Jeremiah 10:14

The contrast is between expensive idols made by a craftsman, who after all that work and expense cannot perform, and plain people whom God makes "in his image" to live to the praise of his glory. There are two kinds of religion, the kind in which we make gods, and the kind in which God makes us.

What are some contemporary idols?

PRAYER: Make me, O God, in your image, after your likeness. Use me for your purposes. Receive me in your mercy and by your grace, in the name and for the sake of Jesus Christ my Lord. *Amen.*

"The Shepherds Are Stupid"
Read Jeremiah 10:17–22

For the shepherds are stupid, and do not
inquire of the Lord; therefore they have
not prospered, and all their flock is
scattered.

Jeremiah 10:21

God wisely provides guides for his people—
prophets, priests, wise men and women—to direct us through the maze of paganism and to train us in the ways of faith. Very frequently, these guides ("shepherds") stupidly abandon their work and go off to do something they think is more urgent and important.

What wise shepherd do you know?

PRAYER: I pray for the shepherds, God: those you have set over your people to lead us beside still waters and in the paths of righteousness. Keep them alert and intelligent, faithful and compassionate, in the name of the Good Shepherd, my Lord and Savior. Amen.

"Not in Their Control"

Read Jeremiah 10:23–25

I know, O Lord, that the way of human
beings is not in their control, that
mortals as they walk cannot direct
their steps.

Jeremiah 10:23

It is neither possible nor desirable that we should
be self-sufficient. We are made in such a way that
we discover the goals of life and the skills of living
by knowing God and believing in him. When we
understand and accept his creation and salvation,
we live well.

What correction has recently helped you?

PRAYER: Daily, dear Lord, I need encouragement,
direction, correction. I look to you for the word
that tells me who I am and where I am going.
"Saviour, like a Shepherd lead us, Much we need
Thy tender care" (Dorothy A. Thrupp, "Saviour,
Like a Shepherd Lead Us," The Hymnbook, 380).
Amen.

"From the Iron-Smelter"
Read Jeremiah 11:1–17

Which I commanded your ancestors when
I brought them out of the land of Egypt,
from the iron-smelter, saying, Listen to
my voice, and do all that I command
you. So shall you be my people, and I
will be your God.

Jeremiah 11:4

Nearly a thousand years before, God had delivered his people from the furnace of Egyptian affliction. Now he is about to plunge them into Babylonian fires of judgment. The warning, "Do not pray for this people," does not mean that there is no hope, but that there is no escape from the chastening judgment.

What will the judgment do to Israel?

PRAYER: As far back as I can see, Lord, I see signs of deliverance and signs of judgment, both of them used for salvation. In times of affliction, you give deliverance; in times of sin, you provide judgment; always your will is done, for which I praise you. *Amen.*

"I Was Like a Gentle Lamb"
Read Jeremiah 11:18–23

But I was like a gentle lamb led to the
slaughter. And I did not know it was
against me that they devised schemes,
saying, "Let us destroy the tree with its
fruit, let us cut him off from the land
of the living, so that his name will no
longer be remembered!"

Jeremiah 11:19

Jeremiah, intent on preaching God's word of judgment, was unaware that the people in his home-
town of Anathoth were plotting his assassination.
But God had promised his prophet protection
(1:18–19), and he kept his promise.

Why did the people want to kill Jeremiah?

PRAYER: Almighty and blessed God, I would, like
Jeremiah, trust your power to deliver me from
unseen dangers and unanticipated malice. I would
live openly and spontaneously, not cautiously and
warily. Deliver me from evil. *Amen.*

"How Will You Compete with Horses?"
Read Jeremiah 12:1–6

> If you have raced with foot-runners and
> they have wearied you, how will you
> compete with horses? And if in a safe
> land you fall down, how will you fare
> in the thickets of the Jordan?
>
> Jeremiah 12:5

Jeremiah's questioning complaint about the prosperity of the wicked (vv. 1–4) meets with a sharp
rebuke from his Lord (vv. 5–6). Instead of a sym-
pathetic, soothing answer, he gets a demanding
challenge: the life of faith is not a bed of roses but
a strenuous contest; the contest has barely begun,
and is Jeremiah ready to give up?

Compare this with Psalm 73.

PRAYER: "Must I be carried to the skies On flowery
beds of ease, While others fought to win the prize,
And sailed through bloody seas?" (Isaac Watts,
"Am I a Soldier of the Cross," *The Hymnbook*, 353).
Amen.

"Birds of Prey"

Read Jeremiah 12:7–13

Is the hyena greedy for my heritage at my
command? Are the birds of prey all
around her? Go, assemble all the wild
animals; bring them to devour her.

Jeremiah 12:9

Judah is different, like a bird of prey. The difference was intended to be a blessing to the nations—like salt, like leaven. Under the conditions
of her rebellion and disobedience, the difference
is only an offense that rouses her neighbors to
anger and attack.

How many times does the word "desolate"
occur?

PRAYER: What difference do you want me to make
among my neighbors this day, Lord? With my co-
workers? In my family? I want to fulfill the special
calling that you have set before me and so be a
blessing to those around me, sharing grace in my
conversation, showing compassion in my acts.
Amen.

"Good for Nothing"
Read Jeremiah 13:1–11

This evil people, who refuse to hear my
words, who stubbornly follow their own
will and have gone after other gods to
serve them and worship them, shall be
like this loincloth, which is good for
nothing.

Jeremiah 13:10

The function of a loincloth is to cleave to the loins
of its owner; the function of Israel was to cleave to
God. But Israel had lost herself by cleaving to idol
worship. Having lost her usefulness, she was "good
for nothing."

What did God make you good for?

PRAYER: Father, I remember my creation in the
image of God. I remember my salvation in the cross
of Jesus. I know I am made to live to your glory and
enjoy you forever. Help me to live up to the dignity
of my creation and salvation. *Amen.*

MARCH 2

"Every Wine-Jar"

Read Jeremiah 13:12–14

> You shall speak to them this word: Thus
> says the Lord, the God of Israel: Every
> wine-jar should be filled with wine. And
> they will say to you, "Do you think we
> do not know that every wine-jar should
> be filled with wine?"
>
> Jeremiah 13:12

The quotation in verse 12 was probably a popular saying: "Let's eat, drink, and be merry—filling ourselves with wine." Jeremiah retorts, "You will be jugs filled with wine all right, but it will be not the wine of merriment but of a drunken stupor. Reeling helplessly as drunken sots, you will smash against each other and be broken."

What makes you happy?

PRAYER: God, I want to be filled with you, not with what the world gives. Nothing but your righteousness can satisfy my hunger and thirst. I would drink deeply of the waters of life and eat with good appetite at the table you set before me. Amen.

"Do Not Be Haughty"
Read Jeremiah 13:15–27

Hear and give ear; do not be haughty,
   for the Lord has spoken.

Jeremiah 13:15

Pride pushes God to the sidelines. The proud do not listen, do not trust, do not love. But no one can live on such terms. The proud are caught up in illusions about themselves and are oblivious to the far greater reality of God. The only way God can rouse them to reality is by a violent rearrangement of the world around them—by judgment.

What does verse 23 mean?

PRAYER: When things go well, Almighty God, I think I can get along without you; and when things go badly, I know I can't. Give me a mustard-seed gift of faith and nurture its tree-sized growth in me, so that I can live habitually sheltered and centered in your grace in Jesus Christ. *Amen.*

"Do Not Forsake Us!"

Read Jeremiah 14:1–10

> Why should you be like someone con-
> fused, like a mighty warrior who cannot
> give help? Yet you, O Lord, are in the
> midst of us, and we are called by your
> name; do not forsake us!
>
> Jeremiah 14:9

Faced with the hardships of drought, the same
people who for years had ignored Jeremiah's passionate preaching suddenly cry out promises of
repentance and petitions for help. But God is not
moved. He will not be used to prop up their fail-
ing standard of living; he will be their Lord or
nothing.

Have you ever been guilty of "foxhole" religion?

PRAYER: I want you, O God, not for occasional
emergencies but as Lord of my life, not to rescue
me from desperate straits but to lead me daily in
paths of righteousness, in the name and for the
sake of Jesus Christ. Amen.

"A Lying Vision"
Read Jeremiah 14:11–16

And the Lord said to me: The prophets are
prophesying lies in my name; I did not
send them, nor did I command them or
speak to them. They are prophesying to
you a lying vision, worthless divination,
and the deceit of their own minds.

Jeremiah 14:14

Often, the main problem in our world is not the
absence of religion but the corruption of religion.
There was plenty of preaching in Israel. But the
preaching was a lie. The prophets preached not
what made the people good but what made them
feel good.

Compare this with chapter 11, verses 14–17.

PRAYER: Empty my mind of "lying visions" and
give me the mind of Christ, O God. Show me
my sin that I may confess it; show me your salvation that I may embrace it. I do not want comfortable, soothing words, but sword-sharp, heart-
penetrating words. *Amen.*

"Have You Completely Rejected?"
Read Jeremiah 14:17–22

Have you completely rejected Judah? Does
your heart loathe Zion? Why have you
struck us down so that there is no healing for us? We look for peace, but find
no good; for a time of healing, but there
is terror instead.

Jeremiah 14:19

The thoroughgoing corruption of priestly and
prophetic religion and the calamitous judgments
of war and disease raised the question of ulti-
macy: "Have you completely rejected?" From that
despairing question, Jeremiah leads the people in
lament, through confession, to the beginnings of
hope (v. 22).

Compare this with Jeremiah 8:22–9:3.

PRAYER: No matter what I see around me, no matter what I feel within me, I will not abandon hope,
Almighty God. I believe that your final word is
salvation; your final verdict, "Well pleased!"; and
your final judgment, "No condemnation." Amen.

"You Are Going Backward"

Read Jeremiah 15:1–9

You have rejected me, says the Lord, you
  are going backward; so I have stretched
  out my hand against you and destroyed
  you—I am weary of relenting.

Jeremiah 15:6

Calamities accumulate. Judgments intensify. God
relentlessly pursues his people. And the people
persist in excluding God from their lives. But no
one can deny God and live. God's judgments are a
massive "no" to a people who are living faith-
lessly and indulgently.

What "no" is God speaking to our world today?

PRAYER: Father in heaven, I don't want to live
backwardly, making useless detours, attempting
futile shortcuts. I want to live in full pursuit of
your ways in Christ, "keeping face forward up the
hill of God" (Walter J. Mathams, "Christ of the
Upward Way," *The Hymnbook*, 295). *Amen.*

"My Wound Incurable"
Read Jeremiah 15:10–18

> Why is my pain unceasing, my wound
> incurable, refusing to be healed? Truly,
> you are to me like a deceitful brook, like
> waters that fail.

Jeremiah 15:18

The people's contempt for God is visited on God's prophet, Jeremiah. He is cursed and isolated. His inner life is a gaping, painful wound. How much can he be expected to take? How much humiliation and rejection can he endure? He lays his questions and his wounds before God in passionate prayer.

What is a "deceitful brook"?

PRAYER: I never like it, Lord, when I experience even a fragment of the hostility and rejection that people direct continuously toward you. Give me the stamina to persevere and the courage to accept my share in the sufferings of my Lord. *Amen.*

"Utter What Is Precious"
Read Jeremiah 15:19–21

Therefore thus says the Lord: If you turn
back, I will take you back, and you shall
stand before me. If you utter what is
precious, and not what is worthless, you
shall serve as my mouth. It is they who
will turn to you, not you who will turn
to them.

Jeremiah 15:19

At the point of despair, tempted to give it all up
and, perhaps, join the ranks of prophets who say
what the people want to hear and bask in their ap-
plause, Jeremiah is fortified by God's promise.
The strengthening word comes when he needs it
most.

Compare this with chapter 1, verse 18.

PRAYER: Faithful Lord, you promised me that no
temptation that comes my way will be stronger
than your provisions for victory over it. Grateful
for your promise, I relax in your faithfulness, sure
of your never-failing help. *Amen.*

MARCH 10

"You Shall Not Take a Wife"
Read Jeremiah 16:1–13

The word of the Lord came to me: You
shall not take a wife, nor shall you have
sons or daughters in this place.

Jeremiah 16:1–2

Jeremiah's life of loneliness was a walking parable
to the people. Uncheered by wife or children, he
was a sign to the nation that all were under the
sentence of doom. Great and small alike would lie
unburied and unlamented.

What else was denied to Jeremiah?

PRAYER: When I, Lord God, blithely ignore the
lonely struggles of those who labor faithfully to
represent your love, forgive me. Help me to share
their burdens and their tears, for Jesus' sake. *Amen.*

"I Will Bring Them Back"
Read Jeremiah 16:14–21

For I will bring them back to their own
land that I gave to their ancestors.

Jeremiah 16:15b

The judgment is stern and absolute. No one will escape. "Fishers" and "hunters" will catch even the most elusive. When caught, we are returned to God's everlasting mercy. A new "exodus" is portrayed for the future (vv. 14–15), after which all nations will respond to God's sovereignty (vv. 19–21).

Where has God found you?

PRAYER: Thank you, God, for hunting me down, for seeking me out, and for bringing me back. Thank you for your persevering mercy and your patient waiting. *Amen.*

"Written with an Iron Pen"
Read Jeremiah 17:1–4

The sin of Judah is written with an iron
  pen; with a diamond point it is engraved
  on the tablet of their hearts, and on the
  horns of their altars.

Jeremiah 17:1

Sin is not a surface blemish. It is chiseled into the
very stuff of our nature. The only treatment for it
is that which God offers. We will not get rid of it
by anything we resolve or propose.

What are Asherim?

PRAYER: You take me much more seriously than I
take myself, great God. You care about the diseased roots of my life, not just its feverish appearance; the ingrained evil, not just the surface disorder. I submit myself to your saving judgment in
the name of Jesus Christ. Amen.

"Blessed Are Those"
Read Jeremiah 17:5–8

Blessed are those who trust in the Lord,
    whose trust is the Lord.

Jeremiah 17:7

A life centered in the human is scrubby and ema-
ciated; a life centered in God is full and vital. Life
is empty when it is empty of God. Nothing can
provide the fullness that we long for—not friends,
not power, not pleasure—but God.

Compare this with Psalm 1.

PRAYER: I receive you, O God, as my Lord and Savior. I receive your blessing, your forgiveness, your
life-renewing spirit. I receive hope and faith and
love. My life is filled with what you give! All
praise to you, great God of grace and glory. *Amen.*

MARCH 14

"The Heart Is Devious"
Read Jeremiah 17:9–10

The heart is devious above all else; it is
    perverse—who can understand it?

                                    Jeremiah 17:9

We don't understand ourselves by looking into
ourselves but by looking to God. The God who
made us and redeemed us knows us better than
we can ever know ourselves. By his Word and
Spirit he instructs us, comprehending our nature
and our destiny.

In what ways is the heart deceitful?

PRAYER: Tell me the truth about myself, God, so
that I can live truly. Show me the reality of my life
so that I can live authentically. Train me in wisdom so that I can live graciously and fully, Christ
living in me. *Amen.*

"Prove to Be Fools"

Read Jeremiah 17:11

> Like the partridge hatching what it did not
> lay, so are all who amass wealth unjustly;
> in mid-life it will leave them, and at
> their end they will prove to be fools.
>
> *Jeremiah 17:11*

A popular proverb of the day held that the partridge gathered chicks from other birds and raised them; since there were no "blood ties," the birds wandered off as soon as they were able. Wealth is like that. If it does not issue from honest work, if there is no natural relation between what we do and what we get, we will be bereft.

What other illustration would suit this truth?

PRAYER: God Almighty, maker of heaven and earth, all things fit into your plan and purpose. Show me how to fit into your design and so participate in the results you destine, reaping and sowing in righteousness. *Amen.*

"Shrine of Our Sanctuary"
Read Jeremiah 17:12–13

O glorious throne, exalted from the
 beginning, shrine of our sanctuary!
Jeremiah 17:12

"Sanctuary is the sense of quietness and of peace.
Overcome in the conflict, bruised and broken in
the battle, the spirit of man flings itself into that
region; and by submission to its law of holiness
and peace, becomes protected from all outside
forces" (G. Campbell Morgan).

Compare this with Revelation 4:2–5.

PRAYER: Throned in splendor, O God, you center
my life and order my days: I praise you for the
blessings and glory that flow into my life, for the
beauty and holiness that are foundations on which
I can live in faith and hope. Amen.

"Heal Me"

Read Jeremiah 17:14–18

Heal me, O Lord, and I shall be healed;
save me, and I shall be saved; for you
are my praise.

Jeremiah 17:14

The taunts of a people who mock his prophetic sermons on judgment lacerate the sensitive spirit of Jeremiah. The wounds are painful, and his faith wavers. The God who commissioned him to such dangerous work must also protect and preserve him in it.

What in you needs healing?

PRAYER: Daily I return to you, merciful Christ, for the help I require to stay healthy in a world of cynicism, disbelief, and dismay. "Heal me, O Lord, and I shall be healed; save me, and I shall be saved; for you are my praise." Amen.

"Keep the Sabbath Day Holy"
Read Jeremiah 17:19–27

And do not carry a burden out of your
houses on the sabbath or do any work,
but keep the sabbath day holy, as I commanded your ancestors.

Jeremiah 17:22

Only when we stop chattering so much can we
hear God speak truly; only when we cease our
frantic activities can we see clearly God's creative
and redemptive work. When we fail to keep the
Sabbath, we fail to realize the centrality of God in
all of life.

How do you keep the Lord's Day holy?

PRAYER: Thank you, Holy Father, for the great gift
of Sabbath, a day of leisure and of silence, a day of
waiting and contemplation, a day of rest and glad-
ness, a day for listening and receiving. *Amen.*

"Like the Clay in the Potter's Hand"
Read Jeremiah 18:1–12

Can I not do with you, O house of Israel,
just as this potter has done? says the
Lord. Just like the clay in the potter's
hand, so are you in my hand, O house
of Israel.

Jeremiah 18:6

This is one of Jeremiah's most famous sermons. In the potter reworking a spoiled vessel until it suits his purpose, he saw a parable of God reworking the spoiled people of Israel into a vessel of redemption.

What else can you learn from the potter's craft?

PRAYER: "Have Thine own way, Lord! Have Thine own way! Thou art the Potter; I am the clay. Mold me and make me After Thy will, While I am waiting, Yielded and still" (Adelaide A. Pollard, "Have Thine Own Way, Lord!" *The Hymnbook*, 302). *Amen.*

"A Most Horrible Thing"
Read Jeremiah 18:13–17

Therefore thus says the Lord: Ask among
the nations: Who has heard the like of
this? The virgin Israel has done a most
horrible thing.

Jeremiah 18:13

Sin is unnatural and irrational. It is a violation of
our created nature; it is an offense to every mature
intelligence. Judgment is God's way of opening
our eyes to the affront and scandal of sin.

Are you horrified by sin?

PRAYER: I am so used to sin, Lord, that I hardly notice its presence. It is so much in the air and prevalent in the landscape that I accept it as normal. By
your word I am learning to recognize how gro-
tesque and monstrous it really is. Show me how to
lead a holy life in Jesus' name. *Amen.*

"Plots Against Jeremiah"
Read Jeremiah 18:18–23

> Then they said, "Come, let us make plots
> against Jeremiah—for instruction shall
> not perish from the priest, nor counsel
> from the wise, nor the word from the
> prophet. Come, let us bring charges
> against him, and let us not heed any
> of his words."
>
> Jeremiah 18:18

Jeremiah was the best friend the people had, but they didn't know it. He preached the truth of God to them, and he interceded with God for them. But the people didn't want God in their lives.

What do you think of Jeremiah's reaction to the plots?

PRAYER: I know, O God, how easy it is to deny what is uncomfortable, to reject what is inconvenient, to plot the elimination of your call to live by faith. But by your grace I will not do it. More than anything, I want you as Lord and Savior of my life. *Amen.*

MARCH 22

"As One Breaks a Potter's Vessel"
Read Jeremiah 19:1–15

And shall say to them: Thus says the Lord of
hosts: So will I break this people and this
city, as one breaks a potter's vessel, so
that it can never be mended. In Topheth
they shall bury until there is no more
room to bury.

Jeremiah 19:11

The clay pot, smashed to pieces before the assembled leaders, made an unforgettable conclusion to Jeremiah's Topheth sermon. No one could ever complain that Jeremiah's preaching failed to hold their attention. No one could complain that his meaning was obscure.

What is the most memorable sermon you have heard?

PRAYER: I thank you, Almighty Father, for all who have spoken your word to me forcibly, directly, plainly. I thank you for their faithfulness and for their vigor, for their courage and their passion. *Amen.*

"Terror-all-around"
Read Jeremiah 20:1–6

The next morning when Pashhur released
  Jeremiah from the stocks, Jeremiah said
  to him, The Lord has named you not
  Pashhur but "Terror-all-around."

Jeremiah 20:3

Physically abused and publicly humiliated, Jeremiah, undaunted, gives Pashhur his true name. Men like Pashhur who drop veils of respectability and well-being over moral and spiritual ugliness are the real threat to society.

Read Jeremiah 6:25, 46:5, and 49:29.

PRAYER: God in Christ, I would be in terror of lies but never of truth, of easy compromises but never of hard commitments, of flattery but never of persecution for the sake of the right. *Amen.*

"I Have Become a Laughingstock"
Read Jeremiah 20:7–13

O Lord, you have enticed me, and I was
  enticed; you have overpowered me, and
  you have prevailed. I have become a
  laughingstock all day long; everyone
  mocks me.

Jeremiah 20:7

The new name that Jeremiah had put on Pashhur,
"Terror-all-around," is now tauntingly thrown
back on Jeremiah, mocking his prophetic seriousness. The people are scornful that anything dread-
ful could take place among citizens as prosperous
and respectable as themselves.

Read Psalm 31:11–13.

PRAYER: God of hosts, when I am plunged into despair by the mincing unconcern, the shallow cynicism, the gossipy self-righteousness of so many, I
need your assurance. Speak peace to my heart;
work salvation in my life. *Amen.*

"Toil and Sorrow"
Read Jeremiah 20:14–18

Why did I come forth from the womb to
see toil and sorrow, and spend my days
in shame?

Jeremiah 20:18

Futility, rejection, humiliation—these can make a
person wish never to have been born. The feelings
are expressed here with passion and vehemence.
Men and women of faith are not strangers to these
feelings, but neither are they abandoned to them.
Dawn breaks. Comfort arrives.

When have you felt like that?

PRAYER: You did it: you changed wild lament into
whirling dance; You ripped off my black mourning band and decked me with wildflowers. I'm
about to burst with song; I can't keep quiet about
you. Yahweh, my God, I can't thank you enough
(Psalm 30:11–12). *Amen.*

MARCH 26

"Say to Zedekiah"
Read Jeremiah 21:1–14

Then Jeremiah said to them: Thus you
shall say to Zedekiah: Thus says the Lord,
the God of Israel: I am going to turn
back the weapons of war that are in your
hands and with which you are fighting
against the king of Babylon and against
the Chaldeans who are besieging you
outside the walls.

Jeremiah 21:3–4a

Was King Zedekiah surprised at the message returned to him from Jeremiah? Probably. He was
used to fawning priests who said what he wanted
to hear. From Jeremiah he heard what God wanted
him to hear.

Whose side is God on?

PRAYER: Just and holy God, give me the honesty
and courage to hear what you speak to me and to
respond to it in repentance and faith. Separate me
from my illusions and fantasies and join me to the
great realities of your righteousness. *Amen.*

"Why Has the Lord Dealt in This Way?"
Read Jeremiah 22:1–9

And many nations will pass by this city,
and all of them will say one to another,
"Why has the Lord dealt in this way
with that great city?"

Jeremiah 22:8

Power and authority must be wedded to morality and righteousness. If they are not—if power becomes violence, if authority becomes arrogance—God's judgment will fell them, as a woodsman fells the choicest cedar.

What ruler will you pray for today?

PRAYER: I pray for those who are in authority in this land, O God, for our president, our legislators, and our judges. Make them wise and just, protect them from lies and corruption, so that we may be blessed with righteousness. *Amen.*

"O Land, Land, Land!"
Read Jeremiah 22:10–30

O land, land, land, hear the word of the
Lord!

Jeremiah 22:29

Three successive kings are personally addressed:
Shallum (v. 11), Jehoiakim (v. 18), and Coniah (v.
24). They were urged to display the cardinal virtue
that was always to distinguish the royal house of
David, namely, to "execute justice and righteousness." Because they failed to do that, they were removed from the land they had been entrusted to
rule.

What political corruption do you find within
yourself?

PRAYER: I listen to your word, Holy Father, directed
to persons who rule and govern—the exposure
of their rapacity and greed, the condemnation of
luxurious sham. The sins I see writ large in them
are also in my heart. I submit to your judgment
and ask for forgiveness. *Amen.*

"A Righteous Branch"
Read Jeremiah 23:1–8

The days are surely coming, says the Lord,
  when I will raise up for David a righteous Branch, and he shall reign as king
  and deal wisely, and shall execute justice
  and righteousness in the land.

Jeremiah 23:5

After the explicit references to the three previous
kings, the implicit reference to the fourth, Zedekiah, is unmistakable. His name meant "the Lord is
my righteousness." But his faithlessness betrayed
the promise of his name. The Lord, in turn, promises a ruler who will execute divine righteousness,
"a righteous Branch."

Who fulfilled the "righteous Branch" prophecy?

PRAYER: How grateful I am, Almighty God, that
no human failures can blot out your promise of
help, no faithlessness erase the evidence of your
faithfulness. Fix my eyes on your presence promised and completed in Jesus Christ. Amen.

"Ungodly"

Read Jeremiah 23:9–15

Both prophet and priest are ungodly;
even in my house I have found their
wickedness, says the Lord.

Jeremiah 23:11

The very persons who were responsible for courageously bringing God's word to the people (the prophets) and the very persons who were responsible for compassionately bringing the people before God (the priests) were self-indulgent and contemptibly timid. It was irresponsibility on a massive scale, and it called for judgment most severe.

What is the difference between Samaria and Jerusalem?

PRAYER: I remember your words, Lord, when you said that to whom much is given, much is required. I know that I have been given much. Keep me true to what you have revealed to me. Make me faithful in witness and love. In Jesus' name. *Amen.*

"Deluding You"
Read Jeremiah 23:16–17

> Thus says the Lord of hosts: Do not listen
> to the words of the prophets who proph-
> esy to you; they are deluding you. They
> speak visions of their own minds, not
> from the mouth of the Lord.
>
> Jeremiah 23:16

The most dangerous lies are religious lies—lies
that separate us from righteousness, lies that mis-
represent sin and dull conscience and excuse irresponsibility. Fed on such lies, we are no longer in
touch with reality.

What religious lies have been told to you?

PRAYER: God, it is hard to hear the truth—and even
harder to respond to it when heard! It is much easier to go along with comfortable lies and sac-
charine flatteries. But I can't live on cotton-candy
religion; feed me on the strong meat of your
gospel. *Amen.*

APRIL 1

"Yet They Ran"
Read Jeremiah 23:18–22

I did not send the prophets, yet they
ran; I did not speak to them, yet they
prophesied.

Jeremiah 23:21

A prophet must be immersed in the word of God
and practiced in the wisdom of God in order to
speak or act rightly. It is not enough to desire to
say kind words; it is not enough to want to do
nice things. It is God's words that must be expressed; it is God's acts that must be witnessed.

What religious activity seems futile to you?

PRAYER: First, O God, I would be still before you,
acquiring a sense of your will, listening to your
life-shaping word, letting myself be moved by
your Spirit. Then, by your grace, I will run in the
way of your commandments. *Amen.*

APRIL 2

"The Burden of the Lord"
Read Jeremiah 23:23–40

> When this people, or a prophet, or a priest asks you, "What is the burden of the Lord?" you shall say to them, "You are the burden, and I will cast you off, says the Lord."
>
> Jeremiah 23:33

"Burden of the Lord," a phrase expressing the awesome gravity of God's concern for the people, had been debased into trite jargon. The solution? Withdraw the phrase from circulation. We must not speak about God in clichés.

What pious clichés can you eliminate from your speech?

PRAYER: God, let my yes be yes and my no, no. Purge my language of pious gossip. Cure me of careless speech and mindless chatter. Especially when I speak of you and to you, I want my words to be accurate and true. *Amen.*

"Two Baskets of Figs"
Read Jeremiah 24:1–10

The Lord showed me two baskets of figs
placed before the temple of the Lord.
Jeremiah 24:1a

Were the people taken into Babylonian exile the
unlucky ones, and the people left in Jerusalem the
lucky ones? Quite the opposite. The exile would
train a people into wholehearted love and service.
Jeremiah's vision shows that what we often imagine to be misfortune may be the best thing that
could happen to us.

What misfortune has God used for your good?

PRAYER: Teach me to interpret events by your
Word, O God, and not by the editorials in the
newspaper. Train me in responding to trouble in
ways that will fix my heart on your salvation, in
the name and for the sake of Jesus Christ my Lord.
Amen.

"Spoken Persistently"

Read Jeremiah 25:1–14

And I have spoken persistently to you, but
you have not listened.

Jeremiah 25:2b

The middle chapter of the book of Jeremiah sum-
marizes twenty-three years of the prophet's preaching and forecasts the seventy years of exile that will
soon begin because the preaching was ignored.

What stands out in Jeremiah's preaching?

PRAYER: I thank you, faithful God, for the persistence of your call to me. Despite my indifference,
you continue to seek me, to invite me, to confront
me. Give me open ears to hear your word and a
new heart to love my Lord and my neighbor. *Amen.*

"The Wine of Wrath"
Read Jeremiah 25:15–38

For thus the Lord, the God of Israel, said to
me: Take from my hand this cup of the
wine of wrath, and make all the nations
to whom I send you drink it.

Jeremiah 25:15

Until now, Jeremiah's preaching has been focused
on Jerusalem; the message is now broadcast in-
ternationally—"all the nations." God's judgment
is compared to a stupefying drink that is passed
around to all the nations.

Compare this with Jeremiah's commission in
chapter 1, verse 5.

PRAYER: Your word, O God, forces me to live in a
world community, aware of all nations, concerned
with all peoples. Thank you for insisting that I
leave the cloistered securities of familiar surround-
ings and experience all your work in all the world.
Amen.

"You Shall Die!"

Read Jeremiah 26:1–19

And when Jeremiah had finished speaking
all that the Lord had commanded him to
speak to all the people, then the priests
and the prophets and all the people laid
hold of him, saying, "You shall die!"

Jeremiah 26:8

Jeremiah's courageous preaching—his famous
temple sermon—nearly cost him his life on this
occasion. But a bold personal defense (vv. 12–15)
and a convincing testimony from friends (vv.
16–19) stayed the execution. Preaching is a haz-
ardous occupation.

What do you know of Micah of Moresheth?

PRAYER: "Are there no foes for me to face? Must I
not stem the flood? Is this vile world a friend to
grace, To help me on to God? Sure I must fight if
I would reign; Increase my courage, Lord; I'll bear
the toil, endure the pain, Supported by Thy
Word" (Isaac Watts, "Am I a Soldier of the Cross,"
The Hymnbook, 353). *Amen.*

"Another Man Prophesying"
Read Jeremiah 26:20–24

There was another man prophesying
in the name of the Lord, Uriah son
of Shemaiah from Kiriath-jearim. He
prophesied against this city and against
this land in words exactly like those of
Jeremiah.

Jeremiah 26:20

Uriah and Jeremiah preached similarly. But when danger threatened, Jeremiah stood his ground and Uriah, in fright, fled to Egypt. Uriah attempted to save his life while Jeremiah gave himself up for dead (v. 14). And Uriah was killed and Jeremiah preserved. "For those who want to save their life will lose it, and those who lose their life for my sake, and for the sake of the gospel, will save it" (Mark 8:35).

Note the reference to Ahikam in 2 Kings 22:12.

PRAYER: God, when I am doing your work, help me to stand my ground, confident that nothing can separate me from your love or your purposes. I want my life to be motivated positively in faith, not negatively in fright; I want to run toward you whom I trust, not away from those whom I fear. Amen.

"Under the Yoke"
Read Jeremiah 27:1–22

I spoke to King Zedekiah of Judah in the
same way: Bring your necks under the
yoke of the king of Babylon, and serve
him and his people, and live.

Jeremiah 27:12

The king of Babylon was God's instrument for
judgment. Rebellion against Nebuchadnezzar was
therefore rebellion against God. It was a particularly
difficult message to accept—God's people being
disciplined by a pagan power?—but for those who
accepted it, it became a way to salvation.

How does this compare or contrast with Jesus'
words in Matthew 11:29–30?

PRAYER: I always prefer soothing words of comfort to blunt words of judgment. I know you
bring comfort, Lord, but I also know you bring
judgment. In faith I would live so that I will receive either at the times you decide are best for
my salvation. *Amen.*

"Listen, Hananiah"
Read Jeremiah 28:1–17

And the prophet Jeremiah said to the
prophet Hananiah, "Listen, Hananiah,
the Lord has not sent you, and you
made this people trust in a lie."

Jeremiah 28:15

The confrontation between the two prophets was
vigorous and colorful. Jeremiah had prophesied a
seventy-year exile (25:11); Hananiah contradicted
him, saying that it would be a mere two years. The
yoke bars—accepted in the one man's trust, broken by the other man's scorn—give visual emphasis to the words.

How were the people to know which message
was true?

PRAYER: Lord, give me a good memory for what is
true in your commandments and for what is essential in your holiness, so that I may respond to
truth and not flattery, to reality and not fantasy.
Amen.

"The Words of the Letter"
Read Jeremiah 29:1—23

These are the words of the letter that the
prophet Jeremiah sent from Jerusalem to
the remaining elders among the exiles,
and to the priests, the prophets, and all
the people, whom Nebuchadnezzar had
taken into exile from Jerusalem to
Babylon.

Jeremiah 29:1

This letter to the exiles is a model of spiritual direction: it encourages the people to accept the conditions of exile and live hopefully and responsibly. They must not live resentfully, cursing their misfortune. And they must not live dreamily, fantasizing a speedy release. God will use the exile to make them whole and blessed.

What letter of personal counsel has made a difference for you?

PRAYER: I thank you, God, for the many ways you employ to direct me: sermons and letters, conversations and examples, old memories and new knowledge. Use all of it to guide me in a growing life of faith, in Christ. *Amen.*

"To Shemaiah"

Read Jeremiah 29:24–32

To Shemaiah of Nehelam you shall say . . .
Jeremiah 29:24

Jeremiah's letter to the exiles provoked an angry response from one of them, Shemaiah. He wants to know why they don't lock up this "madman who prophesies." Even in exile he continues to deny the meaning of judgment.

Compare the false prophets Hananiah (28:17) and Shemaiah.

PRAYER: This world, O God, is no friend to grace. For every word that I hear you speak to me, there are a dozen words of rebuttal from the world. Help me to shut my ears to the world's words and have open ears to your word, in the name of Jesus Christ. *Amen.*

"I Will Bring Them Back"
Read Jeremiah 30:1–3

For the days are surely coming, says the
Lord, when I will restore the fortunes
of my people, Israel and Judah, says the
Lord, and I will bring them back to the
land that I gave to their ancestors and
they shall take possession of it.

Jeremiah 30:3

The next four chapters (30–33) have been de-
scribed with the phrase "the Book of Consolation." Following years of severe judgment preaching, there is this strong message of comfort and
hope. God's last word is not No but Yes.

Compare this with Isaiah 40:1–2.

PRAYER: "O God, who hast willed to restore all
things in Thy beloved Son, the king of all: grant
that the families of the nations, divided and rent
asunder by the wounds of sin, may be subject to his
most gentle rule; who is alive and reigns with Thee
in the unity of the Holy Spirit, one God, world
without end" (*The Book of Common Order*). *Amen.*

"He Shall Be Rescued"
Read Jeremiah 30:4–9

Alas! that day is so great there is none like
   it; it is a time of distress for Jacob; yet he
   shall be rescued from it.

Jeremiah 30:7

The extreme pain and suffering that is being experienced in the judgment is like the pain of childbirth: the pain itself is a sign of new life. When God's judgment comes, it is not a time to throw up our hands in despair, but to lift up our hearts in hope.

What pain in your life is evidence of newly emerging life?

PRAYER: God, I don't want to avoid the pain or deaden the pain that comes when you judge and discipline me. I want to live through it to the new level of salvation to which you are lifting me; in Jesus' name. Amen.

"I Will Heal"

Read Jeremiah 30:10–17

For I will restore health to you, and your
wounds I will heal, says the Lord, because
they have called you an outcast: "It is
Zion; no one cares for her!"

Jeremiah 30:17

Two great facts about Israel describe us all. One,
"no medicine for your wound, no healing for
you"—nothing devised by physicians or politicians will make us whole. Two, "I will restore
health to you"—God cures the incurable; God
uses the act of judgment as a means of salvation.

Compare this with the lament in chapter 8,
verse 22.

PRAYER: Heal the sin-wounds in my life, God, the
parts diseased by disobedience, the parts fractured
by rebellion. Make me whole under your compassionate touch and strengthen me to live in hope
and in love, for Jesus' sake. *Amen.*

"I Am Going to Restore"
Read Jeremiah 30:18–22

Thus says the Lord: I am going to restore
the fortunes of the tents of Jacob, and
have compassion on his dwellings; the
city shall be rebuilt upon its mound, and
the citadel set on its rightful site.

Jeremiah 30:18

Judgment has ravaged the city, turned the temple
into rubble, decimated the population. Salvation
will make a new city and a new people; children
will play and songs will be sung. The worst is
never the last word; the best is.

When was this prophecy fulfilled?

PRAYER: I am all too willing to believe, Lord, that
doomsday is the last word. When I believe that,
everything is tinged with gloom. But time after
time, your Word shows me that resurrection day
is the last word. As I learn to believe that, my days
are bathed in praise. *Amen.*

"Executed and Accomplished"
Read Jeremiah 30:23–24

The fierce anger of the Lord will not turn
back until he has executed and accomplished the intents of his mind. In the
latter days you will understand this.

Jeremiah 30:24

God's will is not a tissue of tentative plans that
may or may not be completed, depending on the
weather or the stock market or public opinion.
"The intents of his mind" finally achieve completed reality. While the work is going on, we
cannot see the result, but we will see it "in the latter days."

Looking back, what can you see completed of
God's work?

PRAYER: "God is working His purpose out As year
succeeds to year: God is working His purpose out,
And the time is drawing near; Nearer and nearer
draws the time, The time that shall surely be,
When the earth shall be filled with the glory of
God As the waters cover the sea" (Arthur Campbell
Ainger, "God Is Working His Purpose Out," The
Hymnbook, 500). Amen.

"Grace in the Wilderness"

Read Jeremiah 31:1–6

At that time, says the Lord, I will be the
God of all the families of Israel, and they
shall be my people. Thus says the Lord:
The people who survived the sword
found grace in the wilderness; when
Israel sought for rest, the Lord appeared
to him from far away.

Jeremiah 31:1–3a

Israel, delivered from Egyptian slavery, found in
the wilderness that God was all-sufficient, that
living by faith put her in touch with the deep realities of God's blessing. Deliverance from Babylonian exile will renew that experience.

How many years separated these two "wilderness experiences"?

PRAYER: Lord God, in the wilderness where I used
to see only emptiness, I am discovering your fullness; in the place where human achievements are
nonexistent, I discover your work in me and know
your blessing. Thank you, God, for grace in the
wilderness. Amen.

"A Great Company"
Read Jeremiah 31:7–9

> See, I am going to bring them from the
>   land of the north, and gather them from
>   the farthest parts of the earth, among
>   them the blind and the lame, those with
>   child and those in labor, together; a
>   great company, they shall return here.
>   Jeremiah 31:8

No matter where or how far away we are scattered in judgment, God will bring us back. No matter how bereft we feel in judgment, we will be restored. No one will be incapacitated for the return; no handicap will eliminate us; no one will be left out.

What is the farthest you have felt from God?

PRAYER: Dear God, there are experiences that seem so devastating that I am sure everything is ruined, that nothing can be restored, nothing salvaged. Then I find that "never" is not a gospel word. Use this vision of restored and praising people for my consolation. *Amen.*

"Radiant over the Goodness"
Read Jeremiah 31:10–14

They shall come and sing aloud on the
height of Zion, and they shall be radiant
over the goodness of the Lord, over the
grain, the wine, and the oil, and over
the young of the flock and the herd;
their life shall become like a watered
garden, and they shall never languish
again.

Jeremiah 31:12

People separated from God's redemption are gathered and restored. Jesus told parables of God seeking the lost sheep, finding the lost coin, welcoming the lost son (Luke 15). Merrymaking, dancing, and joy are what we have to look forward to.

Compare this with Psalm 30.

PRAYER: "Joy of the desolate, Light of the straying, Hope of the penitent, fadeless and pure! Here speaks the Comforter, tenderly saying, 'Earth has no sorrows that heaven cannot cure'" (Thomas Moore, "Come, Ye Disconsolate, Where'er Ye Languish," *The Hymnbook*, 373). *Amen.*

"Rachel Is Weeping"

Read Jeremiah 31:15

Thus says the Lord: A voice is heard in
Ramah, lamentation and bitter weeping.
Rachel is weeping for her children; she
refuses to be comforted for her children,
because they are no more.

Jeremiah 31:15

Rachel's tomb is near Ramah. Her spirit is pictured
haunting her tomb, weeping for her children (she
was Ephraim's grandmother; see v. 18) who had
been deported. It is one of the most heartrending
passages in scripture.

Note the use of this passage in Matthew 2:18.

PRAYER: Lord Jesus, sounds of weeping fill the
pages of scripture and the corridors of history. Sin
has such bitter consequences! Rebellion causes
such endless hurt! Still, I hear your words in the
midst of the laments, "Blessed are those who
mourn for they shall be comforted," and I take
heart. *Amen.*

"Is Ephraim My Dear Son?"

Read Jeremiah 31:16–20

Is Ephraim my dear son? Is he the child
I delight in? As often as I speak against
him, I still remember him. Therefore
I am deeply moved for him; I will surely
have mercy on him, says the Lord.

Jeremiah 31:20

Ephraim, Rachel's grandson (see v. 18), calls out in repentance and is mercifully restored—an old gospel story. Rachel, who thought her sorrow was endless, now has hope. God again does his merciful work of resurrection.

What hope is there in your future?

PRAYER: God, I am always jumping to premature conclusions. I stop in the middle of the story, thinking I can guess the dismal last chapter. But only you can write the conclusion; I believe it to be a conclusion in hope, toward which I will live by your mercy in Jesus Christ. *Amen.*

"Guideposts"
Read Jeremiah 31:21–22

Set up road markers for yourself, make
   yourself guideposts; consider well the
   highway, the road by which you went.
   Return, O virgin Israel, return to these
   your cities.

Jeremiah 31:21

There is a way back to God. Israel doesn't have to
wander around blindly trying this and that road to
see if it might get them to God; the same road that
led to exile, traveled the other direction, will lead
them home.

What are some guideposts marking your pil-
grimage?

PRAYER: "Grace and truth shall mark the way where
the Lord His own will lead, if His word they still
obey and His testimonies heed" (*The Psalter*, 1912).
Amen.

APRIL 23

"My Sleep Was Pleasant"
Read Jeremiah 31:23–26

Thereupon I awoke and looked, and my
   sleep was pleasant to me.

Jeremiah 31:26

This message of hope came in a dream. In the deep, subconscious regions of being, God brings together all the elements of reconstruction so that on waking we are able to greet the day with strength and expectation.

What good dreams have you had recently?

PRAYER: Use my sleeping hours, dear Father, to create wholeness and trust in your all-encompassing purposes. And use my waking hours to lead me, in body and spirit, to obey and love in ways that will bring your purposes into reality. *Amen.*

APRIL 24

"To Build and to Plant"
Read Jeremiah 31:27–30

And just as I have watched over them to
pluck up and break down, to overthrow,
destroy, and bring evil, so I will watch
over them to build and to plant, says the
Lord.

Jeremiah 31:28

The same care that God gives to judgment he gives
to salvation. We must never suppose that judgment
predominates. The work of judgment is only a
prelude to the work of salvation. It is never an end
in itself.

Compare this with chapter 1, verse 10.

PRAYER: God, I thank you that you are a builder
and a planter: that you construct a new way of life
on the rubble of my rebellion, that you grow a life
of righteousness out of the desert of my unbelief.
I delight in your watchful attention and glory in
your ways. *Amen.*

"A New Covenant"
Read Jeremiah 31:31–34

The days are surely coming, says the Lord,
  when I will make a new covenant with
  the house of Israel and the house of
  Judah.

Jeremiah 31:31

God takes over and does perfectly what human beings have bungled badly. What we try to do by our anxious and fatiguing moral effort, namely, get close to God, God graciously creates within our hearts. We are in God's presence by God's act.

What five divine actions ("I will . . .") make up the new covenant?

PRAYER: Thank you, God, for this new covenant, given and completed in Christ. As I receive him by faith, write the ways of truth and grace on my heart, so that I will live deeply and spontaneously a forgiven and praising life. *Amen.*

"This Fixed Order"
Read Jeremiah 31:35–37

If this fixed order were ever to cease from
my presence, says the Lord, then also the
offspring of Israel would cease to be a
nation before me forever.

Jeremiah 31:36

The steady rhythms of creation, the sure rising
of the sun, the dependable arrangements of the
stars—these provide the structure in which the
certain promises of God are worked out, the gracious purposes of Christ accomplished in us.

Why is meditation on creation important?

PRAYER: Use what I can see all around me, Creator
Christ, to convince me of the invisible necessities
of eternity. Make every stone a parable of your
firm foundation, every ray of sunlight a messen-
ger of your penetrating grace. *Amen.*

"Rebuilt for the Lord"

Read Jeremiah 31:38–40

The days are surely coming, says the Lord,
    when the city shall be rebuilt for the
    Lord from the tower of Hananel to the
    Corner Gate.

Jeremiah 31:38

We want to preserve what we have at all costs, supposing that it can never be replaced. We hang on desperately to the status quo, even when it is destroying us. Judgment separates us from those things that obstruct faith and ruin community. What God then rebuilds is better, more extensive, and more lasting than what we had thrown together out of our own faithless anxieties.

What hope do you get from this passage?

PRAYER: Your promises separate me from the false promises of this world, O God. Believing in what you will make of me and my society, I am free to live through the judgment in hope, confident that the days ahead will prosper in a covenant of grace. *Amen.*

"I Bought the Field at Anathoth"
Read Jeremiah 32:1–25

And I bought the field at Anathoth from
my cousin Hanamel, and weighed out
the money to him, seventeen shekels
of silver.

Jeremiah 32:9

While shut up in prison, with the country about
to be overrun by the enemy, Jeremiah purchased
real estate. The act was a convincing demonstration of his hope: he really did believe that God
would restore the land to his people.

How do you express your hope in God's promises?

PRAYER: Like Jeremiah, Lord, I would find everyday ways to express my firm conviction that you
will complete your salvation. I will plan my days
and spend my money in that sure hope, in Jesus'
name. *Amen.*

"Fields Shall Be Bought"
Read Jeremiah 32:26–44

Fields shall be bought for money, and
    deeds shall be signed and sealed and
    witnessed, in the land of Benjamin, in
    the places around Jerusalem, and in the
    cities of Judah, of the hill country, of the
    Shephelah, and of the Negeb; for I will
    restore their fortunes, says the Lord.

Jeremiah 32:44

Jeremiah's act was a prophecy: the widespread
loss and devastation would be succeeded by widespread recovery and restoration. That was God's
promise; God's prophet made it credible by living
out what he was speaking.

What actions demonstrate your beliefs?

PRAYER: So integrate my words and actions, dear
God, that they be always coherent. Let me act
what I believe and believe what I act, both the actions and the beliefs originating in your word to
me in Jesus Christ. Amen.

"Recovery and Healing"
Read Jeremiah 33:1–11

I am going to bring it recovery and
healing; I will heal them and reveal to
them abundance of prosperity and
security.

Jeremiah 33:6

In a prosperous time Jeremiah had been able to discern and articulate dark words of judgment. Now in a dark time he is able to believe and proclaim words of hope. He is not like the sundial that can tell time only when the sun shines; shut up in a dark prison, he is perfectly capable of proclaiming good tidings.

What in your life needs recovery and healing?

PRAYER: Almighty God, let the most important and decisive reality of my life be that you love and that you save me. Let that loom above every unsettling circumstance or bewildering happening. In Jesus' name. *Amen.*

"A Righteous Branch"

Read Jeremiah 33:12–18

> In those days and at that time I will cause
>   a righteous Branch to spring up for
>   David; and he shall execute justice and
>   righteousness in the land.
>
> *Jeremiah 33:15*

Detail after detail are filled into the grand vision of hope. The imagination is provided with specific material to counter the present devastation and rouse a life of faith. Vague longings develop specific expectations: a righteous Lord saves us here and now.

How many details of hope are given?

PRAYER: I praise you for all the promises, O God, and I thank you for bringing them to pass, item by item, in my daily life. What detail will you fill in today? what blessing bestow? what gift deliver? what fruit provide? *Amen.*

"My Covenant with the Day"
Read Jeremiah 33:19–22

> Thus says the Lord: If any of you could
> break my covenant with the day and my
> covenant with the night, so that day and
> night would not come at their appointed
> time, only then could my covenant with
> my servant David be broken, so that he
> would not have a son to reign on his
> throne, and my covenant with my min-
> isters the Levites.
>
> Jeremiah 33:20–21

We often think that the visible world is sure and
dependable, while invisible relations are capri-
cious and chancy. But unseen relations with God
are as sure as night and day. His covenant is as sure
as his creation.

What is the most dependable thing you know?

PRAYER: "New every morning is the love Our
wakening and uprising prove; Thru sleep and darkness safely brought, Restored to life and power and
thought. Only, O Lord, in Thy dear love, Fit us for
perfect rest above, And help us, this and every day,
To live more nearly as we pray" (John Keble, "New
Every Morning Is the Love," The Hymnbook, 45)
Amen.

"Mercy"

Read Jeremiah 33:23–26

For I will restore their fortunes, and will
have mercy upon them.

Jeremiah 33:26b

The last word in this "Book of Consolation" (chaps. 30–33) is *mercy*. Many people had concluded that God had rejected his two families (Israel in the north, Judah in the south) because they experienced the judgment of exile. But judgment is not rejection. Faith sees mercy in God's no as well as in God's yes.

How have you experienced God's mercy in a time of judgment?

PRAYER: "Depth of mercy! can there be Mercy still reserved for me? Can my God His wrath forbear? Me, the chief of sinners, spare? Still for me the Saviour stands, Shows His wounds, and spreads His hands; God is love! I know, I feel; Jesus weeps, and loves me still" (Charles Wesley, "Depth of Mercy! Can There Be," *The Hymnbook*, 273). *Amen.*

"Proclaiming Liberty"

Read Jeremiah 34

You yourselves recently repented and did
what was right in my sight by proclaiming liberty to one another, and you made
a covenant before me in the house that is
called by my name; but then you turned
around and profaned my name when
each of you took back your male and
female slaves.

Jeremiah 34:15–16b

God sets his people free. The theme pervades the
story of God's salvation. The fact of freedom is
God's gift; the use of freedom is our response.
How will we use it? To set others free to live in
praise of God? Or to use others to serve our wants
and desires? When freedom is not shared, it is lost.

How can you extend freedom to others?

PRAYER: I praise you, Father, for the glorious liberty you have provided your children: freedom to
praise, to love, to believe, to hope. In what I do
and say today, help me to extend that freedom
into the lives of those closest to me, setting them
free to live to your glory. Amen.

"The House of the Rechabites"
Read Jeremiah 35

Go to the house of the Rechabites, and
   speak with them, and bring them to
   the house of the Lord, into one of the
   chambers; then offer them wine to
   drink.

Jeremiah 35:2

Is it possible to live a life of obedience? Or is that
expecting too much of mere humans? It is possible. The proof is in the austere and disciplined
Rechabites who, against the stream of custom and
culture, obeyed. If the Rechabites can obey the
commands of a human father, the Israelites can
obey the commands of their heavenly Father. "So
they are without excuse" (Romans 1:20).

Do you think God expects too much of you?

PRAYER: Why am I so content with mediocrities,
with riffraff religion? Why do I live so much of
the time just trying to get by? Lord, forgive my
drifting and apathetic ways and fill me with a zeal
for excellence, for holiness, for the best in obedience and adoration. *Amen.*

"Jeremiah's Dictation"

Read Jeremiah 36

> Then Jeremiah called Baruch son of
> Neriah, and Baruch wrote on a scroll
> at Jeremiah's dictation all the words
> of the Lord that he had spoken to him.
>
> *Jeremiah 36:4*

This is the most detailed account we have of the writing of any part of scripture. Its dictation, transcription, destruction, and rewriting by the prophet Jeremiah, the scribe Baruch, and the flippant king Jehoiakim make a vivid story. These scriptures that are so easily accessible to us were often written and preserved under the most dangerous and dramatic circumstances.

What do you value most about scripture?

PRAYER: "Blessed Lord, who hast caused all holy Scriptures to be written for our learning: grant that we may in such wise hear them, read, mark, learn, and inwardly digest them, that by patience, and comfort of thy holy Word, we may embrace and ever hold fast the blessed hope of everlasting life, which thou hast given us in our Saviour Jesus Christ" (*The Book of Common Worship*). Amen.

"Imprisoned"

Read Jeremiah 37

The officials were enraged at Jeremiah,
  and they beat him and imprisoned him
  in the house of the secretary Jonathan,
  for it had been made a prison.

Jeremiah 37:15

God's people are no strangers to prisons. From patriarchs to prophets to apostles, the prison has frequently been the place of preaching, of praying, of writing. Great words of gospel freedom have been broadcast from these prisons.

Recall some other prison scenes in scripture.

PRAYER: I thank you, God, that nothing can separate me from your love or shut up your purposes. When I am opposed by others and my plans are interrupted by antagonistic wills, show me how to live even more deeply in your will, which cannot be stopped. *Amen.*

"The Cistern of Malchiah"

Read Jeremiah 38

> So they took Jeremiah and threw him into
> the cistern of Malchiah, the king's son,
> which was in the court of the guard,
> letting Jeremiah down by ropes. Now
> there was no water in the cistern, but
> only mud, and Jeremiah sank in the
> mud.
>
> *Jeremiah 38:6*

The passage is marked by contrasts: Jeremiah, muddy from the cistern, and Zedekiah, dressed in royal robes; the prophet, sure and undeviating in his counsel; the king, frightened and nervous over every wisp of rumor. Not our station in life, not our predicament or status, but God's word makes us true.

Read Psalm 40.

PRAYER: God, I am never so far down that I cannot be lifted by your grace; I am never so rejected that I cannot be restored by your comfort; I am never so intimidated that I cannot be made confident by your promise, in Jesus Christ. *Amen.*

"When Jerusalem Was Taken"

Read Jeremiah 39

When Jerusalem was taken, all the officials
of the king of Babylon came and sat in
the middle gate.

Jeremiah 39:3a

The long-prophesied but long-denied event is
accomplished. The willful blindness of Zedekiah
and his predecessors to the signs calling for repentance now becomes an imposed blindness.

What contrasts continue between Jeremiah and
Zedekiah?

PRAYER: I know that there is no avoiding your
word, dear God. What you say comes to pass, soon
or late. What you proclaim comes into being,
judging and saving. By your grace I will live in response to what you say, not in denial of it. *Amen.*

"Gedaliah"

Read Jeremiah 40

Gedaliah son of Ahikam son of Shaphan
    swore to them and their troops, saying,
    "Do not be afraid to serve the Chaldeans.
    Stay in the land and serve the king of
    Babylon, and it shall go well with you."

Jeremiah 40:9

Gedaliah governed the remnant people well. He
persuaded the militant guerrillas in the country-
side to return to farms and vineyards, and he restored order to the country. He was a peaceful man
who won the confidence of those who wanted
peace.

Why do you think Jeremiah chose to stay?

PRAYER: Father in heaven, you provide leaders for
every occasion, and provide the means for your
people to live obediently, even joyfully, in the wake
of judgment. When I come to such places in my
life, prepare me to live so that I will waste no time
in nursing old regrets, but wake each morning
with fresh hope. *Amen.*

"Ishmael"

Read Jeremiah 41

Ishmael son of Nethaniah and the ten
    men with him got up and struck down
    Gedaliah son of Ahikam son of Shaphan
    with the sword and killed him, because
    the king of Babylon had appointed him
    governor in the land.

Jeremiah 41:2

Ishmael apparently was a diehard who fanatically
rejected Jeremiah's interpretation of the Babylonian invasion as God's judgment and thought of it
simply as a violation of personal freedom. His terrorist murderers destroyed everything that had
been recovered since the judgment.

What modern terrorist does this remind you of?

PRAYER: What endless misery comes when your
word is rejected, your grace spurned! God, I want
to learn from your judgments, and I want my
friends to learn from them by the mercy and for
the sake of Jesus Christ. *Amen.*

"Do Not Go to Egypt"

Read Jeremiah 42

The Lord has said to you, O remnant of
Judah, Do not go to Egypt. Be well
aware that I have warned you today
that you have made a fatal mistake.

Jeremiah 42:19–20a

The desire to go to Egypt was understandable: the
continuing threat of Babylon and the anarchy introduced by Ishmael's terrorists made life in Judea
very precarious. But God, with promises of pres-
ervation, commanded them to stay. We do not
learn the will of God by assessing the political cli-
mate.

In what area of your life do you want to know
God's will?

PRAYER: To whom will I listen today, Lord? To the
commentators and editors, the doomsdayers and
forecasters? Or to you? You have given me the desire to know your will; give me also the determined faithfulness to live by it. *Amen.*

"They Did Not Obey"

Read Jeremiah 43

And they came into the land of Egypt,
for they did not obey the voice of the
Lord. And they arrived at Tahpanhes.

Jeremiah 43:7

Johanan chose the way of political expedience, not
obedient faith. He took the remnant to the one
place where he thought they would be safe—to
Egypt. But God's plan for the remnant was in Judea,
not in Egypt. Trying to escape from human violence (Nebuchadnezzar, Ishmael), they ran headlong into God's judgment.

Have you ever asked for advice and not taken it?

PRAYER: My plans, Lord, often seem better to me
than your plans. But they are never whole, as
yours are. Help me to trust and obey your will,
even when it goes against what seems best to me.
Help me to rely on your whole goodness and not
insist on my momentary and partial insights, and
so live by faith and in hope. *Amen.*

"Offerings to the Queen of Heaven"
Read Jeremiah 44

Instead, we will do everything that we have
vowed, make offerings to the queen of
heaven and pour out libations to her,
just as we and our ancestors, our kings
and our officials, used to do in the
towns of Judah and in the streets of
Jerusalem.

Jeremiah 44:17a

Would they, in Egypt, repeat the very sins that had
brought judgment upon them in Judea? They
would; they did. And would God continue to
plead with them in love, correcting, disciplining,
judging? He would; he did.

Compare this with chapter 7, verses 16–20.

PRAYER: Grant, O God, that I will learn from my
mistakes and not senselessly repeat them. Keep
the lessons of my past disobedience fresh in my
conscience so that I may live in a better obedience. Amen.

MAY 15

"Baruch"

Read Jeremiah 45

The word that the prophet Jeremiah spoke
to Baruch son of Neriah, when he wrote
these words in a scroll at the dictation
of Jeremiah, in the fourth year of King
Jehoiakim son of Josiah of Judah:

Jeremiah 45:1

Baruch, faithful scribe to Jeremiah, shared the sufferings of his friend, both spiritual and physical. But he also shared the promises. The hard, perilous, self-effacing work took place in the framework of a sure covenant and an eternal love.

Do you ever "seek great things for yourself"?

PRAYER: As I work today, Father, keep me intent on doing what promotes your will, not what advances me. When it means sharing the sufferings of another, give me strength to do that. When it means subordinating myself to another, give me grace to do that. *Amen.*

MAY 16

"Why Has Apis Fled?"

Read Jeremiah 46

Why has Apis fled? Why did your bull not
  stand?—because the Lord thrust him
  down.

Jeremiah 46:15

Chapters 46–51 are a collection of the messages
that Jeremiah addressed to the surrounding nations. The first message is to Egypt. The sacred
bull, Apis, one of Egypt's prominent gods, was
soon to be toppled by Babylonian armies in the
same judgment that chastened Israel.

In what ways was Egypt important in Israel's
life?

PRAYER: "Lord God of Hosts, whose purpose,
never swerving, Leads toward the day of Jesus
Christ Thy Son, Grant us to march among Thy
faithful legions, Armed with Thy courage, till the
world is won" (Shepherd Knapp, "Lord God of
Hosts, Whose Purpose, Never Swerving," *The
Hymnbook*, 288). *Amen.*

"Baldness Has Come upon Gaza"

Read Jeremiah 47

Baldness has come upon Gaza, Ashkelon
   is silenced. O remnant of their power!
   How long will you gash yourselves?

Jeremiah 47:5

Philistia, the bully aggressor on Israel's flank, challenged the life of faith with brandished swords. The bald heads in Gaza, shaved in grief and shame, will be all that is left of the centuries of vain and strutting defiance.

What stories connected with Philistia do you remember?

PRAYER: I am too often impressed, Lord, by worldly displays of power and too often forgetful that it is not by might or power but by your Spirit that the real work is done in this world. As I observe your judgments on the nations, draw me into a deeper participation in the life of quiet trust and faithful obedience. *Amen.*

"The Pride of Moab"

Read Jeremiah 48

We have heard of the pride of Moab—he is
very proud—of his loftiness, his pride,
and his arrogance, and the haughtiness
of his heart.

Jeremiah 48:29

The chapter is notable for the number of cities
mentioned and the vigor of the images. Moab,
lazy and indolent, proud and arrogant, will be
thoroughly and utterly visited by God. Ignorance
of God does not exempt us from the visitation
of God.

Where was Moab?

PRAYER: "From utmost east to utmost west,
Where'er man's foot hath trod, By the mouth of
many messengers Goes forth the voice of God:
'Give ear to Me, ye continents, Ye isles, give ear
to Me, That the earth may be filled with the glory
of God As the waters cover the sea'" (Arthur
Campbell Ainger, "God Is Working His Purpose
Out," *The Hymnbook*, 500). *Amen.*

"O Daughters of Rabbah! . . . Inhabitants of Dedan!"

Read Jeremiah 49:1–22

Wail, O Heshbon, for Ai is laid waste! Cry out, O daughters of Rabbah! . . . Flee, turn back, get down low, inhabitants of Dedan!

Jeremiah 49:3a, 8a

The sounds of these names fall strange on our ears; many people have never heard them pronounced. These once-proud nations have long been extinct. In Jeremiah's time, they supposed themselves to be safe from foreign attack, impervious to invasion. But neither person nor nation can continue for long in defiance of God.

Where were Ammon and Edom?

PRAYER: "Arm of the Lord, awake, awake! Put on Thy strength, the nations shake, And let the world, adoring, see Triumphs of mercy wrought by Thee" (William Shrubsole, "Arm of the Lord, Awake!" *The Hymnbook*, 497). *Amen.*

"Damascus Has Become Feeble"
Read Jeremiah 49:23–27

Damascus has become feeble, she turned to flee, and panic seized her; anguish and sorrows have taken hold of her, as of a woman in labor.

Jeremiah 49:24

The famous city to the north, Damascus, capital of Syria, once festive with the sights and sounds of robust crowds, is emptied of its vitality as a result of sin. Pride and prowess cannot sustain a civilization.

What associations does Damascus have for you?

PRAYER: Father in heaven, unassisted I can see fine and shimmering displays of achievement all around me. I need your help, though, to see beneath these appearances to the foundations. Is there righteousness there? Justice? Goodness? I want to live a life built on the rock of Christ. *Amen.*

"Advance Against Kedar!"
Read Jeremiah 49:28–33

Concerning Kedar and the kingdoms of
Hazor that King Nebuchadnezzar of
Babylon defeated. Thus says the Lord:
Rise up, advance against Kedar! Destroy
the people of the east!

Jeremiah 49:28

This judgment is delivered against the semino-
madic bedouin of the desert, rather than the city-
dwellers of Damascus. The bedouin's free and
uncomplicated life in the desert brought them no
nearer God. If we do not live in faith, no place we
live can exempt us from God's judgment.

Compare this with Psalm 120.

PRAYER: God, overwhelmed by the frenzy and
complexity of the times in which I live, I look in
envy at simpler cultures and slower-paced times.
But they, too, face judgment. Give me courage to
live entirely in the here and now, not looking over
my shoulder in nostalgia but ahead in hope. *Amen.*

"Break the Bow of Elam"
Read Jeremiah 49:34–39

Thus says the Lord of hosts: I am going to
break the bow of Elam, the mainstay of
their might.

Jeremiah 49:35

The reference to Elam is somewhat of a surprise.
All the other nations that have judgments posted
against them are nations bordering Israel. But
Elam is distant, on the far side of Babylon. Jeremiah's preaching, intensely personal, is never
parochial but widely international.

Note the contrast between verses 35 and 39.

PRAYER: Too often, Father in heaven, I narrow my
interest in your work to what is going on immediately around me. Widen it to include an appreciation for everything you do on "this great roundabout, the world" (William Taylor). *Amen.*

MAY 23

"Babylon Is Taken"

Read Jeremiah 50

Declare among the nations and proclaim,
set up a banner and proclaim, do not
conceal it, say: Babylon is taken, Bel is
put to shame, Merodach is dismayed.
Her images are put to shame, her idols
are dismayed.

Jeremiah 50:2

Babylon is used by God to bring judgment upon
Israel; but Babylon will also experience God's
judgment on herself. Babylon must not suppose
that because she wins a military victory over God's
chosen people, she is being rewarded or is exempt
from God's dealings.

Is there a great nation in our times that you
fear?

PRAYER: God of righteousness and justice, of
mercy and grace, wide-eyed I meditate on your
ways among the nations, on your judgments in
history, on your will accomplished in human affairs, ruling and judging all the earth. I give you
my praise in the name of Jesus Christ. *Amen.*

MAY 24

"Suddenly Babylon Has Fallen"
Read Jeremiah 51:1–58

Suddenly Babylon has fallen and is shattered; wail for her! Bring balm for her
wound; perhaps she may be healed.
Jeremiah 51:8

Babylon represents the organized and vaunting
pride of humanity making a civilization in defiance of, or with indifference toward, God. There
is immense achievement there; there is impressive
power there; there is staggering wealth there. But
God's judgment will level it to the ground and
leave it empty.

Compare this with Revelation 18.

PRAYER: Direct my admiration, Father, toward that
which expresses your goodness and blessing. I am
surrounded by Babylonian excesses and, despite
myself, am often drawn to marvel at them. I need
your daily help to acquire a taste for the simple,
the holy, and the true, especially as it is revealed in
Jesus Christ. *Amen.*

"Seraiah"

Read Jeremiah 51:59–64

And Jeremiah said to Seraiah: "When you
come to Babylon, see that you read all
these words."

Jeremiah 51:61

Jeremiah, unable to travel with the exiles to Babylon, commissioned Seraiah to deliver his prophetic
judgment on arrival. The message was accompa-
nied (a characteristic of Jeremiah's preaching) by a
symbolic act: the Babylonians would both hear
and see the message.

What other "symbol" sermons do you remember?

PRAYER: Almighty God, I thank you for careful,
consistent, and clear revelation, across all these
centuries, making your will plain to all peoples in
all nations. The seed of your word has been faithfully sown. Now, in these last days, bring in a
large and triumphant harvest. Amen.

"He Did What Was Evil"
Read Jeremiah 52:1–11

He did what was evil in the sight of the
Lord, just as Jehoiakim had done.

Jeremiah 52:2

King Zedekiah, set apart for the high task of leading the people, merely represented them, sum-
ming up in his office their rejection of the call to
repentance, and their refusal to submit to the
work of judgment.

What kind of person was Zedekiah?

PRAYER: I pray for the leaders in my government,
O Christ: may they have the courage to stand above
the passions of the people and lead us in ways of
righteousness revealed in your word. *Amen.*

"So Judah Went into Exile"
Read Jeremiah 52:12–30

And the king of Babylon struck them
down, and put them to death at Riblah
in the land of Hamath. So Judah went
into exile out of its land.

Jeremiah 52:27

The long-prophesied but stubbornly disbelieved
judgment is executed. The temple is looted, the
city is burned, the people are marched into exile.
But as catastrophic as the event is, it is not hopeless; for it is God's work, and God will bring salvation out of it.

What work of judgment has changed your life?

PRAYER: "Tie in a living tether The prince and
priest and thrall; Bind all our lives together, Smite
us and save us all; In ire and exultation Aflame
with faith, and free, Lift up a living nation, A single sword to Thee" (G. K. Chesterton, "O God of
Earth and Altar," The Hymnbook, 511). Amen.

"He Spoke Kindly"

Read Jeremiah 52:31–34

He spoke kindly to him, and gave him a
seat above the seats of the other kings
who were with him in Babylon.

Jeremiah 52:32

The fall of Jerusalem is history's testimony that
God's word was fulfilled; the release of King Je-
hoiachin from prison is testimony that it will be
fulfilled—hope will be completed just as surely as
judgment was completed. It is fitting that the last
word in a prophecy so necessarily saturated with
anguish and judgment is a word of freedom and
release.

What signs of hope are there in your life?

PRAYER: God, keep the sequence of your words
straight in my heart: judgment always followed by
salvation; discipline always followed by freedom;
suffering always followed by rejoicing; in the name
of the Father, Son, and Holy Ghost. *Amen.*

"How Lonely Sits the City"

Read Lamentations 1

How lonely sits the city that once was full
of people! How like a widow she has
become, she that was great among the
nations! She that was a princess among
the provinces has become a vassal.

Lamentations 1:1

In 586 B.C. the holy city Jerusalem fell to the
Babylonian armies, as Jeremiah had warned. The
leaders and many of the people were marched six
hundred miles away into exile. It was disaster and
suffering on a monumental scale. Lamentations is
a funeral service for the death of the city.

What is the most extreme instance of suffering
that you know?

PRAYER: You know, God, how diligently I try to
insulate myself from suffering and unhappiness.
But however high I build my defenses, some of it
still gets through. Use these laments and prayers
to train me in meeting sorrow, both mine and
others', courageously, in the name of Jesus. *Amen.*

"The Lord in His Anger"
Read Lamentations 2

> How the Lord in his anger has humiliated
>   daughter Zion! He has thrown down
>   from heaven to earth the splendor of
>   Israel; he has not remembered his foot-
>   stool in the day of his anger.
>
> Lamentations 2:1

The awesome anger of a holy God must never be
interpreted or explained in terms of the petty irri-
tations that pass for anger among us. Insofar as we
face up to and deal with the anger of God, we
grow up in faith and learn the meaning of his love,
which suffers and saves.

How many times does the word "anger" appear in these verses?

PRAYER: Deliver me, O holy Father, from fairy-tale
religions that deny your majesty, avoid your holiness, and pretend that your anger is only a childish misunderstanding on my part that I will grow
out of. In Jesus' name. *Amen.*

"I Am One Who Has Seen Affliction"
Read Lamentations 3

I am one who has seen affliction under the
   rod of God's wrath.

Lamentations 3:1

Images of punishment, illness, war, imprisonment,
and wild beasts are used to express the complexity
and terror of suffering. Putting a name to pain is a
first step in recovery from it. The metaphors give
handles to the suffering so that it can be grasped
and handed over to God.

What image best expresses your experience in
suffering?

PRAYER: I know, Lord Jesus Christ, that you have
been through it all, experienced all pain and overcome all suffering. Confidently, I trust you to
work out your purposes in my life, sure that nothing can separate me from your love. Amen.

JUNE 1

"The Gold Has Grown Dim"
Read Lamentations 4

How the gold has grown dim, how the
 pure gold is changed! The sacred stones
 lie scattered at the head of every street.
Lamentations 4:1

It is not possible to appreciate, or sometimes even
to see, wholeness in the world when sin-suffering
overwhelms the soul. Punishing guilt throws a
shroud of despair over everything: "How the pure
gold is changed!"

What has happened to Jerusalem?

PRAYER: Father, I don't want to look at your world
through self-deluding rose-colored glasses, or
through smoked-glass despair. Provide me with a
clear lens of faith through which I can see judgment and accept forgiveness. *Amen.*

JUNE 2

"Remember, O Lord"
Read Lamentations 5

Remember, O Lord, what has befallen us;
  look, and see our disgrace!

Lamentations 5:1

The ultimate language of suffering is prayer, for it
is God, finally, with whom we have to do. Putting
our suffering before God does two things: it makes
him companion to our suffering: it invites his redemption from our suffering.

How does prayer change suffering?

PRAYER: God, in the closed-up attics of memory I
have old and musty leftovers of guilt and wrong,
of hurt and bitterness: let the breeze of your Spirit
blow through me, airing me out and cleaning me
up for love and praise, in Jesus Christ. *Amen.*

"Nebuchadnezzar"

Read Daniel 1:1–2

In the third year of the reign of
King Jehoiakim of Judah, King
Nebuchadnezzar of Babylon came
to Jerusalem and besieged it.

Daniel 1:1

Nebuchadnezzar was a servant of God but he never knew it. He thought he was making his mark as a great king by conquering the Jews; in fact, he was making the Jews a great people by putting them through a testing that refined and matured them.

What do you know about Nebuchadnezzar?

PRAYER: God Almighty, you rule the nations still, and in spite of every obstacle and all rebellion, you invade the world with love and mercy. I give you praise and thanks that no one, whether he or she knows it or not, lives untouched by your grace. Do your will in others' lives and in mine. Amen.

JUNE 4

"Without Physical Defect"
Read Daniel 1:3–5

Young men without physical defect and
handsome, versed in every branch of
wisdom, endowed with knowledge and
insight, and competent to serve in the
king's palace; they were to be taught the
literature and language of the Chaldeans.
Daniel 1:4

The best of Israel had been taken into exile; now
the best of these were chosen to serve the king: he
wanted the very best in servants! Well educated,
carefully groomed, deeply cultured. We are going
to see how the most selfish of motives will be
used by a kindly Providence.

What do you know about the exile?

PRAYER: God, instead of getting angry at the way
other people try to use me and shape me to their
purposes, I want to discover how you weave their
actions into the great tapestry of your perfect will.
Amen.

"Among Them Were Daniel"
Read Daniel 1:6–7

Among them were Daniel, Hananiah,
    Mishael, and Azariah, from the tribe
    of Judah.

Daniel 1:6

Daniel's name means "God renders the verdict."
Daniel in exile was evidence of God's judgment on
Israel; Daniel in exile was also evidence of God's
judgment on Babylon. Daniel is a spotlighted instance of God making decisions in history.

Why were the names changed?

PRAYER: Father, write your new name in my heart:
establish your identity deep within me, so that
everything I think and say and do may be a working out of what you have created. *Amen.*

"They Appeared Better"
Read Daniel 1:8–16

At the end of ten days it was observed that
they appeared better and fatter than all
the young men who had been eating the
royal rations.

Daniel 1:15

If Daniel and his friends were to be of use to God
in the Babylonian court, they had to retain their
distinctive commitments. They could have, in contrast to their less fortunate colleagues, indulged
themselves in the lap of luxury. They chose to discipline their appetites and maintain continuity with
their own people.

Does your diet reflect your commitments and
values?

PRAYER: I want everything I do, Lord, including
the decisions I make about the food I eat, to be a
means of living to your glory. I don't want to live
in mindless gluttony but in considerate gratitude,
appreciative and thoughtful for everything you set
before me. *Amen.*

"God Gave Knowledge and Skill"
Read Daniel 1:17–19

To these four young men God gave
knowledge and skill in every aspect
of literature and wisdom; Daniel also
had insight into all visions and dreams.

Daniel 1:17

In the midst of pressures to conform and embrace
the Babylonian fashion, the four youths stay true
to their origins and stick to their values. Because
they do, God is able to fashion skilled and learned
witnesses. God has infiltrated the pagan court with
his agents!

What skills has God given you?

PRAYER: I am caught between a desire to please my
peers and a hunger after your righteousness, O
God: give me the courage to choose your truth
and refuse the shifting fashions of the age, in Jesus'
name. Amen.

JUNE 8

"Ten Times Better"
Read Daniel 1:20–21

> In every matter of wisdom and under-
> standing concerning which the king
> inquired of them, he found them ten
> times better than all the magicians and
> enchanters in his whole kingdom.
>
> Daniel 1:20

The ways in which God equips us, both physically
and morally, are far superior to the world's ways.
Commitments are far better than self-indulgences;
humility in prayer is always better than the arrogance of magic. And sometimes even the rulers of
this world recognize the superiority of God's ways.

What is better about God's methods of educat-
ing us?

PRAYER: I submit myself to your word, Almighty
God, and learn of truth and peace and judgment.
I learn, not to become accredited by the world for
its honors, but to become of use to you for the
work of justice and the life of salvation. *Amen.*

"Nebuchadnezzar Dreamed"
Read Daniel 2:1–11

In the second year of Nebuchadnezzar's reign, Nebuchadnezzar dreamed such dreams that his spirit was troubled and his sleep left him.

Daniel 2:1

The king took his dreams seriously and wanted to know their meaning. But he also understood that his advisers could manipulate their interpretations (the interpretation of dreams is a notoriously subjective business) to their purposes. He set these impossible conditions to avenge himself on their relentless court intrigues.

Do you take your dreams seriously?

PRAYER: Lord God of all peoples and nations, the conditions that look impossible to me are opportunities for you; show me how to live obediently in the midst of what I don't understand, so that I may share the solution you are working out by grace, in Christ. *Amen.*

"Daniel Responded with Prudence"
Read Daniel 2:12–16

Then Daniel responded with prudence
and discretion to Arioch, the king's
chief executioner, who had gone out
to execute the wise men of Babylon.
Daniel 2:14

Daniel and his friends were lumped with all the
wise men under sentence of death. Far from pan-
icking, Daniel discerned that God's purposes were
being worked out. Instead of frantically looking
for ways of escape, he asked to be brought to the
very king who had ordered his death.

What is your first response to trouble?

PRAYER: Father, when every circumstance seems
overwhelmingly against me and I see no way out,
create hope and trust in me, so that I am ready for
what you will create by your Holy Spirit. Amen.

"Seek Mercy"

Read Daniel 2:17–23

And told them to seek mercy from the God
of heaven concerning this mystery, so
that Daniel and his companions with the
rest of the wise men of Babylon might
not perish.

Daniel 2:18

Daniel is at the center of this story, but he is not there by himself. His three friends are companions in prayer as well as in danger. Instead of spending the night in sleepless anxiety, they joined in intercession before God.

Who prays with and for you?

PRAYER: So many things I do not understand, O God! So many complexities that baffle me! I wait before you, expectant of your revelation that shows me that your will is done and that your kingdom comes. *Amen.*

"But There Is a God"
Read Daniel 2:24–30

But there is a God in heaven who reveals
   mysteries, and he has disclosed to King
   Nebuchadnezzar what will happen at the
   end of days. Your dream and the visions
   of your head as you lay in bed were
   these . . .

Daniel 2:28

Daniel had already received God's interpretation.
He could have used it to elevate himself to a place
of prominence, but he chose to give witness to his
God. It is not so much the king's dream that is interpreted—that is mere scaffolding—as the gospel
of God that is proclaimed.

Why was Arioch in a hurry?

PRAYER: God, it is so easy to use the life of faith to
my own advantages; help me to maintain obedience so that it is used to share your good news of
mercy and love. Let me never interpret salvation
as mere self-preservation. *Amen.*

"The Great God Has Informed"
Read Daniel 2:31–45

The great God has informed the king what
shall be hereafter. The dream is certain,
and its interpretation trustworthy.
Daniel 2:45b

The dream and its interpretation provide a sweeping view of history: human kingdoms are in de-
cline; God's kingdom will be established forever.
The purpose of the dream is to shift the center of
trust from what we do to what God does.

How does our government compare to God's
rule?

PRAYER: God, you are king forever: I entrust myself to your rule and mercy. I set myself under
your command, glad to serve you in devout obedience, in the name of Jesus Christ. *Amen.*

"Promoted Daniel"

Read Daniel 2:46–49

Then the king promoted Daniel, gave him
many great gifts, and made him ruler
over the whole province of Babylon and
chief prefect over all the wise men of
Babylon.

Daniel 2:48

Overnight, Daniel was elevated from obscure slavery to honored authority. But it was not Daniel so much as the God he served who was honored. It was Daniel's relationship to the "revealer of mysteries" that was introduced into the nation's affairs.

Compare this with Psalm 75:6–7.

PRAYER: Father in heaven, I accept the place where you have put me as the right place for service. Show me how to be faithful and diligent in the work you have provided for me, caring only for the reward that you provide. *Amen.*

"Worship the Golden Statue"

Read Daniel 3:1–7

That when you hear the sound of the horn, pipe, lyre, trigon, harp, drum, and entire musical ensemble, you are to fall down and worship the golden statue that King Nebuchadnezzar has set up.

Daniel 3:5

It is a common affliction of people in power: they are not content to rule but want to be worshiped as well. They are not satisfied with respect; they want adoration.

What are some of the golden images in our times?

PRAYER: There are so many images set up around me, Lord, and so many invitations to worship! In this world full of fraudulent gods and goddesses, help me to keep all my worship for you and you alone. *Amen.*

"Certain Jews"

Read Daniel 3:8–12

There are certain Jews whom you have
appointed over the affairs of the province of Babylon: Shadrach, Meshach,
and Abednego. These pay no heed to
you, O King. They do not serve your
gods and they do not worship the
golden statue that you have set up.

Daniel 3:12

One thing is shown clearly in the accusation:
Daniel and his friends had not changed a bit,
though their circumstances had changed markedly.
They were loyal to their God when they were
slaves; they were loyal to their God when they were
honored. Their lives were centered in God, not politics.

Do external circumstances influence your relationship with God?

PRAYER: God, I want to live steadfastly in faith. I
don't want to be blown by every wind, tossed by
every wave. Train me in the ways of discipleship
so that I serve you well in all kinds of weather. Amen.

"Able to Deliver"

Read Daniel 3:13–18

If our God whom we serve is able to
deliver us from the furnace of blazing
fire and out of your hand, O king,
let him deliver us.

Daniel 3:17

The three men believed that God could save them
from anything, but their loyalty was not contin-
gent on their rescue. They will not defect in their
worship of God, regardless of the consequences
to them.

How do you account for the Jews' strength?

PRAYER: The relationship that I have with you,
Almighty God, means more to me than anything
else. Let nothing this day diminish my trust or divert my obedience. In every test, keep me true, in
the name and for the sake of Jesus Christ. Amen.

"Four Men Unbound"

Read Daniel 3:19–25

He replied, "But I see four men unbound,
    walking in the middle of the fire, and
    they are not hurt; and the fourth has the
    appearance of a god."

Daniel 3:25

The story of the fiery furnace has captured the imagination of the devout. It inspires steadfastness generation after generation. It witnesses to hope in the worst of circumstances. The great thing is not that the story is remembered, but that it is re-experienced.

Who was the fourth person?

PRAYER: Lord, thank you for good stories to remember and tell. I am even more thankful that I can live the stories myself, experiencing the visitations of your Spirit in my times of need. *Amen.*

"No Other God Who Is Able"
Read Daniel 3:26–30

Therefore I make a decree: Any people,
nation, or language that utters blas-
phemy against the God of Shadrach,
Meshach, and Abednego shall be torn
limb from limb, and their houses laid
in ruins; for there is no other god who
is able to deliver in this way.

Daniel 3:29

The king honored the bravery of the three men,
but better yet, he recognized the God in whose
service they were brave. In the confused religious
world of gods and goddesses, their witness provided clear access to the true God.

What brave witnesses have influenced you?

PRAYER: God of strength and glory, who delivers
from sin and death, let me live this day in courageous and consistent witness to your power to save.
Amen.

JUNE 20

"A Tree"

Read Daniel 4:1–18

Upon my bed this is what I saw; there was
   a tree at the center of the earth, and its
   height was great.

Daniel 4:10

The king's dream of a tree brings Daniel, once
again, to a place of witness. Unfortunately, the
king seems to have little interest in God except
when he is puzzled or distressed.

What makes you think of God?

PRAYER: You are, O God, closer than breathing,
nearer than hands and feet, yet I am often negli-
gent of your presence, forgetful of your word. Remind and revive me so that I may live every day
alert and believing, responsive to all that you are
to me in Jesus Christ. *Amen.*

"Atone for Your Sins"

Read Daniel 4:19–27

Therefore, O king, may my counsel be
acceptable to you: atone for your sins
with righteousness, and your iniquities
with mercy to the oppressed, so that
your prosperity may be prolonged.

Daniel 4:27

In Daniel's interpretation, the dream is not a pre-
diction but a warning. The dream does not announce what is fated; rather, Daniel uses it to
persuade the king to acknowledge that God rules,
and to change his cruel and immoral government
into a reign of righteousness.

What is the key sentence in the interpretation?

PRAYER: I want to know many things, O God, but
I want to change very little. I want to know what
will happen. I am not nearly as interested in finding out how I can make a difference. Forgive me
for being merely curious, when I should be living
courageously. *Amen.*

"Until You Have Learned"
Read Daniel 4:28–33

You shall be driven away from human
society, and your dwelling shall be
with the animals of the field. You shall
be made to eat grass like oxen, and
seven times shall pass over you, until
you have learned that the Most High
has sovereignty over the kingdom of
mortals and gives it to whom he will.

Daniel 4:32

God has his own educational style: if we will not
learn by warning, we will learn through hard circumstances. The judgment on the king taught
him how ludicrous his pretensions to majesty
were.

What have you learned from God's judgment?

PRAYER: What do you have to teach me today, Lord
God? How will you use the circumstances of these
next hours to train me in a recognition of your
majesty and a life of faith and hope and love? *Amen.*

"My Reason Returned to Me"

Read Daniel 4:34–37

When that period was over, I, Nebuchadnezzar, lifted my eyes to heaven, and
my reason returned to me. I blessed the
Most High, and praised and honored
the one who lives forever. For his sovereignty is an everlasting sovereignty, and
his kingdom endures from generation
to generation.

Daniel 4:34

When we try to be more than human beings, we
become less. In attempting to live like a god, Nebuchadnezzar actually took on the appearance and
behavior of a brute. He became truly himself again
when he worshiped and walked humbly with his
God.

How do you best express humanness?

PRAYER: "Blessing and honor and glory and power,
Wisdom and riches and strength evermore Give ye
to Him who our battle hath won, Whose are the
Kingdom, the crown, and the throne" (Horatius
Bonar, "Blessing and Honor and Glory and Power,"
The Hymnbook, 137). Amen.

"His Knees Knocked Together"
Read Daniel 5:1–9

Then the king's face turned pale, and his
thoughts terrified him. His limbs gave
way, and his knees knocked together.

Daniel 5:6

The banquet seems to have been a deliberate sac-
rilege, using the sacred vessels from Jerusalem for
a drunken carouse in Babylon. The king's terror is
evidence of an awareness that he was violating sacred things—that he had gone too far and was
now faced with God's judgment.

What makes you afraid?

PRAYER: Let me, Holy God, never treat lightly any
part of this creation that you have set apart for acts
of love and mercy and peace. I want to look at
everything and everyone that comes my way, things
and people, with a sense of reverence and praise.
Amen.

"Let Daniel Be Called"

Read Daniel 5:10–12

Now let Daniel be called, and he will give
the interpretation.

Daniel 5:12b

Memories are short. What the father learned, the
son forgot. Every generation begins anew to learn
its place before God. Fortunately, we do not have
to start from scratch; there are Daniels around who
bridge the gaps in our experience and memory.

What wise person do you trust?

PRAYER: Keep me in touch, gracious God, with
wise and experienced guides in the faith, so that
whenever I am plunged into perplexity or bewildered by doubt, I may be led and taught into a
deeper maturity in Christ. *Amen.*

JUNE 26

"Though You Knew All This"
Read Daniel 5:13–28

And you, Belshazzar his son, have not
   humbled your heart, even though you
   knew all this!

Daniel 5:22

Belshazzar's forgetfulness was not mental, but
moral. Although he knew the facts of the past, he
had not lived their meaning. Daniel's message is
not a generalized essay on right and wrong, but a
personal application of God's rule in the immedi-
ate present.

What do you know that you do not live?

PRAYER: Father in heaven, I know so much more
in my head than I have taken into my heart. Train
me in the ways of speech and behavior that put
your truth into living action, through the power
of the Holy Spirit. *Amen.*

"That Very Night"
Read Daniel 5:29–31

That very night Belshazzar, the Chaldean
king, was killed.

Daniel 5:30

Belshazzar apparently accepted Daniel's message,
since he rewarded him lavishly, but he procrasti-
nated his response to it. Scripture warns us re-
peatedly, however, not to delay. We do not know
when death will come, only that it will come.

Do you think often about your death?

PRAYER: "Teach me to live, that I may dread The
grave as little as my bed; Teach me to die, that so I
may Rise glorious at the Judgment Day" (Thomas
Ken, "All Praise to Thee, My God, This Night," *The
Hymnbook*, 63). *Amen.*

JUNE 28

"Grounds for Complaint"
Read Daniel 6:1–9

So the presidents and the satraps tried to
  find grounds for complaint against
  Daniel in connection with the kingdom.
  But they could find no grounds for complaint or any corruption, because he was
  faithful, and no negligence or corruption could be found in him.

Daniel 6:4

Jealousy is a vicious sin. The jealous person cannot bear to admit excellence in another. The
motto is, If I have to be a molehill, I'll use my pick
and shovel to get rid of all the mountains.

Is there anyone of whom you are jealous?

PRAYER: Gracious and Almighty God, give me a
spirit of appreciation and generosity so that I can
respond to every beauty in others, every achievement in my friends, with praise and celebration.
Amen.

JUNE 29

"Down on His Knees"
Read Daniel 6:10–15

> Although Daniel knew that the document
> had been signed, he continued to go to
> his house, which had windows in its
> upper room open toward Jerusalem, and
> to get down on his knees three times a
> day to pray to his God and praise him,
> just as he had done previously.
>
> Daniel 6:10

Prayer, for Daniel, was not an intermittent whim
but an uninterrupted commitment. His relationship with God, nurtured and deepened in habitual
prayer, centered his existence. The edict of Darius
and the jealousy of the courtiers were minor background incidents to this great passion.

When and why do you pray?

PRAYER: On my knees before you, O Christ, I am
in place to know your will and my need: mercifully direct and graciously strengthen me through
the coming hours so that I may live with purpose
and ardor to the glory of your name. *Amen.*

"Into the Den of Lions"

Read Daniel 6:16–18

Then the king gave the command, and
Daniel was brought and thrown into the
den of lions. The king said to Daniel,
"May your God, whom you faithfully
serve, deliver you!"

Daniel 6:16

Daniel in the lions' den holds a central place in the
Christian memory: we know that there is no danger that cannot be survived by the person of faith;
we know that those who are steadfast in God have
nothing to fear from human cruelty or animal bru-
tality. Whether we live or die, we are the Lord's.

How do you account for Darius's concern?

PRAYER: I give up too easily, O God: hostile threats
intimidate me; pessimistic forecasts depress me;
the world's ways demoralize me. Give me the courage of Daniel—the ability to live by faith as a mi-
nority, if need be, through Him who strengthens
me. Amen.

JULY 1

"My God Sent His Angel"
Read Daniel 6:19–24

My God sent his angel and shut the lions'
   mouths so that they would not hurt me,
   because I was found blameless before
   him; and also before you, O king, I have
   done no wrong.

Daniel 6:22

We are not always able to observe the symmetry
of justice as dramatized here in the vindication
of Daniel and the punishment of his accusers. But
the symmetry is there, whether we see it or not.
In God's moral universe, all evil and every goodness find their proper conclusion in the grand
scheme of redemption.

Compare this with Romans 8:37–39.

PRAYER: My trust is in you, Almighty God, as you
work your purposes out in this disordered world.
I live not by what I see, but by what I believe,
quite sure that the judge of all the earth does right,
through Jesus Christ. Amen.

"He Delivers and Rescues"
Read Daniel 6:25–28

He delivers and rescues, he works signs
and wonders in heaven and on earth;
for he has saved Daniel from the power
of the lions.

Daniel 6:27

The great heart of the biblical message is that God
delivers: he is not only great in himself, but he is
also great on behalf of us. He enters into history
and does for us what we cannot do for ourselves.

What does it mean to be saved?

PRAYER: "Praise we God the only Son, Who in
mercy sought us; Born to save a world undone, Out
of death He brought us; Here awhile He showed
His love, Suffered uncomplaining, Now He pleads
for us above, Risen, ascended reigning!" (Cyril A.
Alington, "Come, Ye People, Rise and Sing," *The
Hymnbook*, 39). *Amen.*

"A Dream and Visions"

Read Daniel 7:1–10

In the first year of King Belshazzar of Babylon, Daniel had a dream and visions of his head as he lay in bed. Then he wrote down the dream.

Daniel 7:1

The second half of Daniel (chaps. 7–12) is a series of dreams and visions that establish the certainty of God's rule in the midst of the cruel and unjust rulers of history. This first vision clearly sets God's dazzling and magnificent judgment over the "beast" politics of history.

What are the characteristics of the four beast-kingdoms?

PRAYER: God, glorious and holy, too often I know you only as Lord of my life, but not also as Lord of all the kingdoms of the earth. Through Daniel's visions and dreams, stretch my understanding so that I respond in praise to your rule over all places and peoples, through Christ the Lord. *Amen.*

"One Like a Human Being"
Read Daniel 7:11–14

> As I watched in the night visions I saw
> one like a human being coming with
> the clouds of heaven. And he came to
> the Ancient One and was presented
> before him.
>
> Daniel 7:13

A second figure appears in the vision: "one like a human being." In addition to the majestic rule of the Ancient of Days, there is redemption to be accomplished by the Son of man, as fallen humanity is restored to fellowship with God. "Son of man" was one of Jesus' favorite titles for himself.

Can you find places where Jesus used this title?

PRAYER: "O Son of Man, our Hero strong and tender, Whose servants are the brave in all the earth, Our living sacrifice to Thee we render, Who sharest all our sorrows, all our mirth" (Frank Fletcher, "O Son of Man, Our Hero Strong and Tender," *The Hymnbook*, 217). Amen.

"The Truth Concerning All This"
Read Daniel 7:15–18

> I approached one of the attendants to ask
> him the truth concerning all this. So he
> said that he would disclose to me the
> interpretation of the matter.
>
> Daniel 7:16

The four kings are contrasted with the saints of
the Most High. There are two kinds of rule: rule
by political power and rule by faithful goodness.
Daniel's vision is a powerful witness to the superiority of right over might.

What did Jesus say about the kingdom?

PRAYER: God, capture my imagination with a vision of your rule and my place in it. When I am
intimidated by world political forces, show me
how to participate in the deep, underground spiritual energies that flow from your throne. Amen.

"Holy Ones of the Most High"
Read Daniel 7·19–27

But the holy ones of the Most High shall
receive the kingdom and possess the
kingdom forever—forever and ever.

Daniel 7:18

The kingdom of the fourth beast is, clearly, a for-
midable kingdom. Whichever historical nation it
refers to, the message is clear: the most elaborate
political system that human beings can construct
is no match for the kingdom that God will finally
give to his people.

How would you identify the fourth beast-
nation?

PRAYER: I don't see any way in which I can amount
to anything or influence anyone in the super-
power politics of the world, Almighty God. Still,
your vision to Daniel shows people like me not as
pawns of history but as rulers in eternity. In light
of that, help me to live, even now, responsibly as
a future ruler, not listlessly or fatalistically. Amen.

JULY 7

"The Account Ends"

Read Daniel 7:28

Here the account ends. As for me, Daniel,
my thoughts greatly terrified me, and
my face turned pale; but I kept the
matter in my mind.

Daniel 7:28

History is an arena noisy with conflict. Nations, like rams and goats, charge and destroy each other. In the midst of it all, it appears that truth is trampled in the dust. But that is not the reality: God's holiness will be visibly and triumphantly restored in our midst.

What nations do you think these beasts refer to?

PRAYER: "Though the cause of evil prosper, Yet 'tis truth alone is strong; Though her portion be the scaffold, And upon the throne be wrong, Yet that scaffold sways the future, And, behind the dim unknown, Standeth God within the shadow Keeping watch above His own" (James Russell Lowell, "Once to Every Man and Nation," *The Hymnbook*, 361). *Amen.*

"It Cast Truth to the Ground"
Read Daniel 8:1–14

Because of wickedness, the host was given
  over to it together with the regular burnt
  offering; it cast truth to the ground, and
  kept prospering in what it did.

Daniel 8:12

Horns dominate this passage. The horn is a symbol of power—in this case, arrogant, God-defying, truth-despising power. The vaunted "horns" of history swell into prominence, destroy, and are, in turn, destroyed. All the while, the scorned and trampled sanctuary, the place of worship, is being prepared for restoration—for resurrection.

How many times does the word "horn(s)" occur in these verses?

PRAYER: God Almighty, strong to save, keep me quietly centered in the sanctuary where I am directed to adore and submit to your powerful Spirit; and keep me unimpressed by the conspicuous "horns" of history that magnify themselves and bring nothing but desolation. *Amen.*

"I Tried to Understand It"
Read Daniel 8:15–17

When I, Daniel, had seen the vision,
   I tried to understand it. Then someone
   appeared standing before me, having
   the appearance of a man.

Daniel 8:15

"The end is where we start from" (T. S. Eliot). The end is not only terminus, it is purposed goal. By understanding the direction of history, we learn how to direct our lives in God's ways.

Whom else did Gabriel appear to?

PRAYER: Lord Jesus Christ, help me to keep my eyes on the goal where you draw all things to yourself, so that I will run with enduring patience, avoiding all detours and rejecting all distraction. *Amen.*

"Not by Human Hands"
Read Daniel 8:18–26

By his cunning he shall make deceit
prosper under his hand, and in his own
mind he shall be great. Without warning
he shall destroy many and shall even rise
up against the Prince of princes. But he
shall be broken, and not by human
hands.

Daniel 8:25

Although an interpretation of history is given, the
main thrust of this vision is a spiritual strategy:
the godless and defiant powers of this world will
not be put down by human power but by divine
will.

What influences you most in your understanding of politics?

PRAYER: Almighty Savior, I want to live alertly and
responsibly as a citizen of this land, but I want
even more to live devoutly and passionately as a
believer in your rule. Show me how to keep my
priorities straight and my trust secure. Amen.

"About the King's Business"

Read Daniel 8:27

So I, Daniel, was overcome and lay sick for
some days; then I arose and went about
the king's business. But I was dismayed
by the vision and did not understand it.

Daniel 8:27

Daniel knew that he was in a key position; his
sense of the divine will in his life was strong. All
the same, though, he was bewildered as to what
the prophetic visions intended. But he didn't quit
when he didn't understand; he continued to live
responsibly and openly toward God's direction.

What do you do when you are bewildered?

PRAYER: You commended, Lord, those who believe without seeing. There are many things I don't
see. Often, in the day-by-day confusion, I fail to
put it all together. But confident of the scriptures
that show you working all things well in history, I
live in praise. *Amen.*

"The Devastation of Jerusalem"

Read Daniel 9:1–2

In the first year of his reign, I, Daniel,
perceived in the books the number of
years that, according to the word of the
Lord to the prophet Jeremiah, must be
fulfilled for the devastation of Jerusalem,
namely, seventy years.

Daniel 9:2

The prophet not only makes scripture, he reads scripture. Out of what God has said he discovers what God will do. Scripture reading is no academic exercise but a living involvement in God's action.

What is your most recent discovery in reading scripture?

PRAYER: I open this book of scripture, God, listening for your word: speak your words of truth to me—the great realities of the past, but also the greater realities that you are now continuing in this world in my life. *Amen.*

"Confession"

Read Daniel 9:3–19

Then I turned to the Lord God, to seek an
answer by prayer and supplication with
fasting and sackcloth and ashes. I prayed
to the Lord my God and made
confession.

Daniel 9:3–4a

This great prayer of confession intercedes for the
salvation of the people. There is no argument with
God, no pleading a case, only an immense sense of
sin with no hope except on the grounds of mercy.

What are the key words in the prayer?

PRAYER: Lord Jesus Christ, prayers like this bring
me up short and show me the trivial and superficial ways in which I live: take me to the depths of
my sin, and to the greater depths of your mercy,
where I live by grace. *Amen.*

"Came to Me in Swift Flight"
Read Daniel 9:20–23

> While I was speaking in prayer, the man
> Gabriel, whom I had seen before in a
> vision, came to me in swift flight at the
> time of the evening sacrifice.
>
> Daniel 9:21

This is one of the great biblical representations of answered prayer. God speeds his answers to us. His first word is that we are "greatly beloved." In that intimacy he teaches us his salvation and gives us understanding.

What is the emphasis of the answer?

PRAYER: Lord, I have never seen Gabriel but I believe in his ministry—the swift representation of your listening love, the quick response of your understanding compassion. By faith and not by faith, I will live in your answering grace. *Amen.*

"Desolations Are Decreed"
Read Daniel 9:24–27

After the sixty-two weeks, an anointed one
   shall be cut off and shall have nothing,
   and the troops of the prince who is to
   come shall destroy the city and the sanctuary. Its end shall come with a flood,
   and to the end there shall be war. Deso-
   lations are decreed.

Daniel 9:26

The prophetic insight into the future always en-
genders hope: God will complete his purposes.
But it is not Pollyannaish—there is much suffering to experience, many judgments to be endured.
Scripture prepares us for difficult times by building hopeful endurance in us.

How do you understand the numbers here?

PRAYER: I know it does no good, God, to just hope
that things will get better, for sometimes they get
worse. But the worse, I see, is part of your plan
too, which will become, finally, your best in Christ.
Amen.

"A Great Conflict"

Read Daniel 10:1

In the third year of King Cyrus of Persia,
    a word was revealed to Daniel, who was
    named Belteshazzar. The word was true,
    and it concerned a great conflict. He
    understood the word, having received
    understanding in the vision.

Daniel 10:1

The vocation of prophet was (is) both difficult and dangerous. It would be much easier to be a professional soother of the social conscience. But among a people rebellious against God, God struggles to win them to faith and love. Truth does not soothe untruth but challenges it.

What truth challenges you to change?

PRAYER: I don't want, O Christ, just words that make me feel better but your word that makes us better, even when it means painful changing and difficult repentance. *Amen.*

"A Man Clothed in Linen"
Read Daniel 10:2–9

I looked up and saw a man clothed in
linen, with a belt of gold from Uphaz
around his waist.

Daniel 10:5

Like Paul on the road to Damascus, Daniel sees a
vision that is withheld from his companions, the
impact of which throws him to the ground un-
conscious. One of our poets said that we cannot
bear very much reality. God's presence is overwhelming.

Compare this with Revelation 1:13–14.

PRAYER: Distracted and inattentive, I miss the signs
of your glory, O God. But many have not missed
them—so many of your servants have been caught
and arrested by the vision of your being there with
them. I will live in praise and in response to their
witness. Amen.

"Stand on Your Feet"
Read Daniel 10:10–14

He said to me, "Daniel, greatly beloved,
pay attention to the words that I am
going to speak to you. Stand on your
feet, for I have now been sent to you."
Daniel 10:11a

God does not leave us prostrate or paralyzed: we
are touched and energized and commissioned.
Each of us, like Daniel, has work to do and a command
to obey. It is a great encouragement to know
that we are backed up by the angels "quick to hear
and do what he says" (Psalm 103:20).

Compare this with Revelation 1:17–20.

PRAYER: I hardly dare to believe, gracious Lord,
that you take the time to answer my prayers. Still,
the evidence is powerful that you do. I will, then,
continue to pray and believe and obey. *Amen.*

"Touched My Lips"
Read Daniel 10:15–17

Then one in human form touched my lips,
and I opened my mouth to speak, and
said to the one who stood before me,
"My lord, because of the vision such
pains have come upon me that I retain
no strength."

Daniel 10:16

A sense of inadequacy is common among biblical witnesses: Moses and Jeremiah and Isaiah were sure that they could not speak God's word. But they could. God equips us for what he commissions us.

Compare this with Isaiah 6:1–9.

PRAYER: Holy Father, the more I know myself, the more I realize that I am ill-equipped to speak in truth or act in love. But the more I know you, the more I find that you have ways of bringing strength out of weakness. Thank you. *Amen.*

"Michael, Your Prince"
Read Daniel 10:18–21

But I am to tell you what is inscribed in
the book of truth. There is no one with
me who contends against these princes
except Michael, your prince.

Daniel 10:21

Persia and Greece were, successively, the greatest
powers the world had seen. But there were greater
powers by far working behind the scenes. The
archangels Gabriel and Michael (and how many
others?), whose names are not entered in history
books, shaped the course of history.

What do you know about angels?

PRAYER: "Mighty God, while angels bless Thee,
May a mortal sing Thy name? Lord of men as well
as angels, Thou art every creature's theme. Lord of
every land and nation, Ancient of eternal days,
Sounded thru the wide creation Be Thy just and
endless praise" (Robert Robinson, "Mighty God,
While Angels Bless Thee," The Hymnbook, 10). Amen.

"Support and Strengthen"

Read Daniel 11:1

As for me, in the first year of Darius
the Mede, I stood up to support and
strengthen him.

Daniel 11:1

Whatever the content of the prophet's speech, the
purpose is positive. God's word, rightly applied,
brings the best out of us and establishes the best
in us. Whether Darius knew it or not, Daniel was
the best ally he had.

Compare this with 1 Corinthians 15:58.

PRAYER: Lord God, as I study and comprehend your
Word, show me how to use it in my relationships
with those over and around me to affirm them in
your good purposes, and so promote righteousness for your sake. *Amen.*

"His Kingdom Shall Be Broken"
Read Daniel 11:2–4

And while still rising in power, his kingdom shall be broken and divided toward
the four winds of heaven, but not to his
posterity, nor according to the dominion
with which he ruled; for his kingdom
shall be uprooted and go to others
besides these.

Daniel 11:4

In this commentary on world politics, one meaning is clear: the greatest ruler cannot make his will
effective for long. As soon as he is dead, everything
is scattered to the four winds. Implicit is a contrast
with God's will, which works through the generations a constant design of redemption.

What political forces is God involved in today?

PRAYER: God Almighty, use this message to train
me in looking at the world's affairs. Keep me responsible in praying for the leaders and loyal to
your will as expressed in Jesus Christ, who is King
of kings and Lord of lords. *Amen.*

"Shall Not Endure"

Read Daniel 11:5–6

But she shall not retain her power, and his
    offspring shall not endure. She shall be
    given up, she and her attendants and her
    child and the one who supported her.

Daniel 11:6b

Alliances are the stuff of world politics—patch-
works of compromises and agreements that attempt to balance and control self-interest. But
they never last. Someone's weakness is always exposed and explicated. God's kingdom works dif-
ferently—not through quicksand alliances but on
a rock-sure covenant.

What is God's covenant?

PRAYER: I trust myself to your government, God,
knowing that when I am weak you do not take advantage of me but use your strength to support
and guide me. *Amen.*

"King of the North . . . King of the South"
Read Daniel 11:7–9

For some years he shall refrain from attack-
ing the king of the north; then the latter
shall invade the realm of the king of the
south, but will return to his own land.

Daniel 11:8b–9

Through much of their existence, God's people
were swept back and forth by power struggles between nations north and south. But they never lost
their identity. Always, God's purposes were revealed in them. They were spiritual giants among
the pygmy politicians who strutted in the north
and in the south.

Who wields world power today?

PRAYER: As impressive as the world powers are,
dear God, and as arresting as the headlines of their
activities are, I choose to put my trust in you, invisible and unobtrusive. *Amen.*

"He Shall Not Prevail"
Read Daniel 11:10–13

When the multitude has been carried off,
his heart shall be exalted, and he shall
overthrow tens of thousands, but he
shall not prevail.

Daniel 11:12

The balance of power seesaws back and forth between north (Syria) and south (Egypt). There is no permanence on the basis of military power. No one wins a war. History is a textbook of the foolishness of "Might is right."

How many wars have you known in your lifetime?

PRAYER: God of glory, when so many try to find ways of getting what they want through violence, train me in the ways of peace, so that I can be among those who live in your kingdom of love and justice. *Amen.*

"An End to His Insolence"
Read Daniel 11:14–19

Afterward he shall turn to the coast-
lands, and shall capture many. But a
commander shall put an end to his
insolence; indeed, he shall turn his
insolence back upon him.

Daniel 11:18

Reading Daniel is like reading the daily newspaper: it tells of the intrigues of the so-called powerful who are out to grab everything they can get.
The person of faith, sure that God is sovereign,
can afford to take a bemused look at it all.

What nations show insolence today?

PRAYER: When the mood of the age tempts me to
put myself first and my interests convince me that
my desires are preeminent, I need your counsel,
Lord, to learn reconciliation in which your will is
primary and your love has the highest value. *Amen.*

"A Contemptible Person"

Read Daniel 11:20–28

> In his place shall arise a contemptible
> person on whom royal majesty had
> not been conferred; he shall come
> in without warning and obtain the
> kingdom through intrigue.
>
> Daniel 11:21

One king came to power who fits Daniel's description—Antiochus Epiphenes. His rapacious arrogance and villainy mark him as a representative of all who defy God and despise holy things.

Who is the most evil ruler you can think of?

PRAYER: Holy God, history is full of men who supposed that because they were kings they could act like gods. Not one of them was able to do it. Every one fell apart at the last. Only you, O God, are holy and good: all praise to your great name. Amen.

"The Abomination That Makes Desolate"

Read Daniel 11:29–35

> Forces sent by him shall occupy and
> profane the temple and fortress. They
> shall abolish the regular burnt offering
> and set up the abomination that makes
> desolate.
>
> *Daniel 11:31*

An actual incident is specified here: Antiochus, the evil king, desecrated the altar in the Jerusalem temple by sacrificing pigs on it in 168 B.C. The center of worship for God's people was deliberately and outrageously violated.

Note Jesus' use of this expression in Matthew 24:15.

PRAYER: Lord God Almighty, prepare me even now for the worst that can come into my life. Ground me so deeply in your mercy and love that nothing humankind can do will be able to shake my trust in your righteous rule. *Amen.*

"Consider Himself Greater"
Read Daniel 11:36–39

> The king shall act as he pleases. He shall
> exalt himself and consider himself
> greater than any god, and shall speak
> horrendous things against the God of
> gods. He shall prosper until the period
> of wrath is completed, for what is
> determined shall be done.
>
> Daniel 11:36

Frequently, maybe always, politics competes with
religion in order to promise, if not a life beyond,
"then a new deal on this earth, and a Leader
smiling charismatically from the placards" (Erik
Erikson).

What political promises interfere with your
faith?

PRAYER: It would be so much easier, God, to put
my faith in the politicians—if they would only
deliver on what they promised! Show me how to
give to Caesar what is Caesar's and to you what is
yours and only yours. *Amen.*

"Come to His End"

Read Daniel 11:40–45

He shall pitch his palatial tents between
the sea and the beautiful holy mountain.
Yet he shall come to his end, with no
one to help him.

Daniel 11:45

There are earthly kingdoms that look absolutely invincible, splendid, and glorious. But in historical fact they are extremely short-lived. Prophetic scripture trains us to take lightly every political power and to live, regardless of appearances and despite the cost, in loyalty to God's rule.

What earthly powers have you seen fall?

PRAYER: "Crowns and thrones may perish, Kingdoms rise and wane, But the Church of Jesus Constant will remain; Gates of hell can never 'gainst that Church prevail; we have Christ's own promise, And that cannot fail" (Sabine Baring-Gould, "Onward, Christian Soldiers," The Hymnbook, 350). Amen.

"Shall Be Delivered"

Read Daniel 12:1–2

At that time Michael, the great prince,
    the protector of your people, shall arise.
    There shall be a time of anguish, such
    as has never occurred since nations first
    came into existence. But at that time
    your people shall be delivered, everyone
    who is found written in the book.

Daniel 12:1

The decisive battles are fought in the heavens; the victories are transferred to earth. Michael is more than a match for any earthly army. God's people have a champion whose victory prize is eternal life.

Compare this with Revelation 12.

PRAYER: Lord God of hosts, I am confident of victory, not mine but yours, which will include all that you intended in my creation and salvation through Jesus Christ. *Amen.*

AUGUST 1

"Running Back and Forth"
Read Daniel 12:3–4

But you, Daniel, keep the words secret
   and the book sealed until the time of
   the end. Many shall be running back
   and forth, and evil shall increase.

Daniel 12:4

Going faster will not improve our position if we
have lost our sense of direction. Accumulating
facts will not tell us the meaning of life if we have
no way to interpret them.

How do you get your sense of direction?

PRAYER: Great and gracious God, thank you for a
clear goal in Jesus Christ and a clear revelation in
Christ so that I know both who I am and where I
am going. *Amen.*

"At the End"

Read Daniel 12:5–13

> But you, go your way, and rest; you shall
> rise for your reward at the end of the
> days.

Daniel 12:13

Every story needs an ending: life does not meander aimlessly; the soul is not rudderless. Daniel's strong sense of finish helps us live with present uncertainties without panic and without despair.

What do you hope most for in the future?

PRAYER: Eternal God, as I am in the middle of the journey, steady my pace and give me daily strength. "I do not ask to see the distant scene—one step enough for me" (John Henry Newman, "Lead, Kindly Light," *The Hymnbook*, 331). *Amen.*

AUGUST 3

"The Lord Said to Hosea"

Read Hosea 1:1–3

When the Lord first spoke through Hosea,
the Lord said to Hosea, "Go, take for
yourself a wife of whoredom and have
children of whoredom, for the land
commits great whoredom by forsaking
the Lord."

Hosea 1:2

God's commitment to and covenant with Israel,
and her unfaithfulness and its consequences, are
experienced personally and dramatized publicly
in Hosea's actual marriage to Gomer, a woman
notorious for her "running around."

Do you know anything about Hosea? What?

PRAYER: God of the prophets, you used Hosea to
both act out and speak your mighty and gracious
word. Now give me observing eyes and attentive
ears, so that as I meditate on his ministry I may
grow into a better discipleship, through Jesus
Christ. Amen.

"Name Him Jezreel"

Read Hosea 1:4–5

And the Lord said to him, "Name him
  Jezreel; for in a little while I will punish
  the house of Jehu for the blood of
  Jezreel, and I will put an end to the
  kingdom of the house of Israel."

Hosea 1:4

Jezreel was the name of one of the capitals of King
Ahab and his notoriously wicked consort, Jezebel.
As such, it had been a concentration of bloody vio-
lence. Hosea's son is a walking reminder that God
has not forgotten—he will do something about
Jezreel.

What do you remember about Ahab and Jezebel?

PRAYER: "From all that terror teaches, From lies
of tongue and pen; From all the easy speeches
That comfort cruel men; From sale and profanation Of honor and the sword; From sleep and
from damnation, Deliver us, good Lord!" (G. K.
Chesterton, "O God of Earth and Altar," *The Hymnbook*, 511). *Amen.*

"No Longer Have Pity"

Read Hosea 1:6–9

She conceived again and bore a daughter.
   Then the Lord said to him, "Name her
   Lo-ruhamah, for I will no longer have
   pity on the house of Israel or forgive
   them."

Hosea 1:6

There were people in Hosea's time (as in our own) who were saying, "I like to sin, God likes to forgive: the world is admirably arranged" (W. H. Auden). The name of Hosea's daughter is a rebuke to such presumptuousness.

What would it feel like to be "no longer pitied"?

PRAYER: God, grant that I will never look on your compassion and forgiveness as something I deserve; that I will never lose sight of the immense cost that you paid in Jesus to redeem me from my sins. *Amen.*

"Children of the Living God"

Read Hosea 1:10–11

Yet the number of the people of Israel shall
be like the sand of the sea, which can
be neither measured nor numbered; and
in the place where it was said to them,
"You are not my people," it shall be said
to them, "Children of the living God."

Hosea 1:10

Hosea's three children demonstrate the consequences of unfaithfulness. But God will demonstrate something else—he will start over with them, dramatizing forgiveness and forming a new people, "children of the living God."

Review the names of Hosea's three children, why are they important?

PRAYER: Eternal Father, you never seem to run out of ways to circumvent my disobedience. No matter what I do, you come up with new ways of showing me you can forgive me and save me in Jesus Christ. Thank you. Amen.

"Plead with Your Mother"
Read Hosea 2:1–5

Plead with your mother, plead—for she is
not my wife, and I am not her husband—
that she put away her whoring from her
face, and her adultery from between her
breasts.

Hosea 2:2

The nation Israel, like the wife Gomer, has abandoned commitment to the one who loved her and
has gone with anyone who promised excitement
or material gain. For both nation and woman, it
is a way of life that will put her, finally, in the
"wilderness."

How do you know that God loves you?

PRAYER: When I realize how steadily and strongly
you love me, O God, I am more determined than
ever to honor your love, to be faithful to your covenant with me, and to respond to your will for
me, through Jesus Christ my Lord. *Amen.*

"Hedge Up Her Way"
Read Hosea 2:6–9

Therefore I will hedge up her way with
thorns; and I will build a wall against
her, so that she cannot find her paths.

Hosea 2:6

Mercifully, God does not permit us to run unobstructed in ways that lead to destruction. He sets up roadblocks that force us to reassess our position, thereby providing opportunities for us to repent and return to his way, which leads to life.

Have you ever had a disappointment, a "setback," that stimulated new growth in the Lord?

PRAYER: Father, thank you for the interruptions and frustrations that you introduce into my life when I depart from your will. I complain at the time, but afterward I'm grateful. Receive my thanks in Jesus' name. *Amen.*

AUGUST 9

"An End to All Her Mirth"
Read Hosea 2:10–13

I will put an end to all her mirth, her
festivals, her new moons, her sabbaths,
and all her appointed festivals.

Hosea 2:11

A massive propaganda entices us to do wrong because "it is more fun." The promise of pleasure
lures many into sinful ways. But God prevents it
by withdrawing the experience of joy in order to
drive us back to himself.

Is God against having fun?

PRAYER: When I try to get joy or pleasure in a way
that avoids your presence, O Lord, stop me so that
I can find a way back to your Son who will make
my joy full. Amen.

"I Will Now Allure Her"
Read Hosea 2:14–15

Therefore, I will now allure her,
    and bring her into the wilderness,
    and speak tenderly to her.

Hosea 2:14

God's strategy is to bring his unfaithful people back to the place of the honeymoon, the wilderness. In that setting, his words of tenderness will arouse the old associations of first love when God and Israel were bound together in a covenant of life.

Recall the time when you first became a Christian.

PRAYER: O God of love, let me get the full impact of your wooing words, realizing the seriousness and persistence of your commitment to me, and so experience with my whole person the meaning of the love you have shown in Jesus Christ. *Amen.*

"My Husband"

Read Hosea 2:16–20

On that day, says the Lord, you will call
  me, "My husband," and no longer will
  you call me, "My Baal."

Hosea 2:16

Christians are the "bride"—God is the "husband."
But what kind of husband? A husband who, like
"Baal," owns the wife as a piece of property and
orders her around? No—a real husband who enters into loyal covenant with his wife and treats her
with respect as a person.

Compare this with Ephesians 5:23–27.

PRAYER: God, you have better ways of being my
Lord and Master than anything I ever supposed.
What has become hackneyed and decadent under
centuries of sin is transformed by your tenderness, so that I learn what it means to be loved by
a God of salvation. All praise to you in Jesus
Christ! Amen.

"On That Day"

Read Hosea 2:21–23

On that day I will answer, says the Lord,
I will answer the heavens and they shall
answer the earth.

Hosea 2:21

The disharmonies that sin introduced into the world, disrupting nature, morals, and spirit, are all reversed by God's redemption. There will be a perfect correspondence between what God wants and what we, his people, desire.

When do you think "that day" is?

PRAYER: "I am Thine, O Lord, I have heard Thy voice, And it told Thy love to me; But I long to rise in the arms of faith, And be closer drawn to Thee. Draw me nearer, nearer, blessed Lord, To the cross where Thou has died; Draw me nearer, nearer, nearer blessed Lord, To Thy precious, bleeding side" (Fanny Crosby, "I Am Thine, O Lord," *The Hymnbook*, 320). *Amen.*

"I Bought Her"

Read Hosea 3:1–5

So I bought her for fifteen shekels of silver
    and a homer of barley and a measure
    of wine.

Hosea 3:2

Gomer, Hosea's wife, is unfaithful to him and finally becomes a slave-prostitute. Hosea goes to the slave market and buys her back, restoring her to full status as a wife again—just as God goes after his unfaithful people, "buys" them back in redemption, and accepts them.

How does God "buy" us back?

PRAYER: Dear God, the astounding persistence of your love for me makes resistance futile. I run from you, avoid you, deny you—and still you find ways to convincingly love me. And now I am learning to love in return through Jesus Christ. *Amen.*

"The Land Mourns"

Read Hosea 4:1–6

Therefore the land mourns, and all who
live in it languish; together with the
wild animals and the birds of the air,
even the fish of the sea are perishing.

Hosea 4:3

Sin is not a private matter between humanity and
God; it is a public matter of creation and government. So deeply is the created world disrupted by
moral and spiritual wrong that even the "land
mourns."

How many sins are listed? Do they still occur?

PRAYER: Almighty God, you created this magnificent world, every part of it designed to express
your love and fulfill your purpose, and I think I
can use it to play out my petty games. Forgive me
for the galling presumption that sets aside your
great plan for my ignorant whims. In Jesus' name.
Amen.

"They Feed on the Sin"

Read Hosea 4:7–10

They feed on the sin of my people;
they are greedy for their iniquity.

Hosea 4:8

The more sin there was, the more business the priests had. It was to their advantage to keep the people ignorant and retain all the power in their hands. The very ones who ought to have been getting the people close to God were, in fact, acting as a barrier.

Read Hebrews 7:26–28 for a different description of a priest.

PRAYER: How glad I am, Father, for the new priest you sent, "not a high priest who is unable to sympathize with our weaknesses, but one who in every respect has been tempted as we are, yet without sinning" (Hebrews 4:15), even Jesus Christ. *Amen.*

"A People Without Understanding"
Read Hosea 4:11–14

I will not punish your daughters when they
play the whore, nor your daughters-in-
law when they commit adultery; for the
men themselves go aside with whores,
and sacrifice with temple prostitutes;
thus a people without understanding
comes to ruin.

Hosea 4:14

The religion of the day was one of feeling rather
than of understanding. The people did what felt
good when they felt like doing it. Adequate, perhaps, for animals, but not for human beings who
have minds to share God's thoughts and wills to
respond to his purposes.

Do you ever have to choose between *feeling* good
and *being* good?

PRAYER: You have commanded me, O God, to love
you "with all my heart and with all my soul and
with all my might" (Deuteronomy 6:4)—every
part of me, from my instincts to my intelligence.
Help me to do it to the glory of your name. *Amen.*

"A Stubborn Heifer"

Read Hosea 4:15–19

Like a stubborn heifer, Israel is stubborn;
    can the Lord now feed them like a lamb
    in a broad pasture?

Hosea 4:16

The usual animal image for the people of God is "sheep." Though sheep go astray, they can at least be led—they will follow a good shepherd. But these people are stubborn and balky. What can be done with them? They seem hopeless.

Do any of your actions betray an inward stubbornness to God?

PRAYER: God, I want to be what you want me to be: open and responsive to your word, quick to forsake my sins and learn your righteousness, through Jesus Christ, "that great shepherd of the sheep" (*The Book of Common Worship*). *Amen.*

"The Spirit of Whoredom"
Read Hosea 5:1–4

Their deeds do not permit them to return
to their God. For the spirit of whoredom
is within them, and they do not know
the Lord.

Hosea 5:4

Both the priests and the people are guilty: the priests have given bad leadership; the people have been more than willing to follow it. The "spirit of whoredom"—contempt for loyal commitment to God combined with a restless pursuit of satisfaction with any number of gods and goddesses—has taken over.

What result does the "spirit of whoredom" have?

PRAYER: "Come, Holy Ghost, our souls inspire, And lighten with celestial fire; Thou the anointing Spirit art, Who dost Thy sevenfold gifts impart. Praise to Thy eternal merit, Father, Son, and Holy Spirit" (Old plainsong, "Come, Holy Ghost, Our Souls Inspire," *The Hymnbook*, 237). *Amen.*

"They Will Not Find Him"
Read Hosea 5:5–7

With their flocks and herds they shall go
to seek the Lord, but they will not find
him; he has withdrawn from them.

Hosea 5:6

God is not an object, one more god among the
idols, that can be searched for and found at human beings' pleasure. He is available to neither
the curious nor the fickle. He is *person*, and can be
known only through personal commitment—that
is, in faith.

Do you find God or does God find you?

PRAYER: O God, with this dread sentence before
me, "he has withdrawn from them," I am well
warned. Prevent me from ever coming to you
simply as diversion or as last resort. I want to
learn constancy and love after the manner of my
Lord and Savior. *Amen.*

"Sound the Alarm"
Read Hosea 5:8–12

Blow the horn in Gibeah, the trumpet in
   Ramah. Sound the alarm at Beth-aven;
   look behind you, Benjamin!

Hosea 5:8

The prophet is like a man who, when he notices a
fire in a building, pulls the fire alarm that will
warn the inhabitants and get help. The purpose of
the alarm is not to gather a crowd to watch a spec-
tacular blaze. The purpose is rescue.

Upon whom do you depend to warn you of
danger?

PRAYER: Father, when I hear your prophetic warnings, may I not look around for someone else to
whom they more obviously refer, but examine
my own heart, accept your judgment, and receive
your salvation, through Jesus Christ. *Amen.*

"Not Able to Cure You"

Read Hosea 5:13–14

When Ephraim saw his sickness, and
   Judah his wound, then Ephraim went
   to Assyria, and sent to the great king.
   But he is not able to cure you or heal
   your wound.

Hosea 5:13

The sin-caused sickness of the nation sent its people looking for a cure. But they went to the wrong place—they went to the "quack doctor" Assyria. He was impressive and famous, but absolutely incompetent in matters of righteousness and justice.

What are some popular "solutions" to what is wrong with the world?

PRAYER: When I, Lord, try to get a quick and easy cure for what is wrong with my life without returning to you, frustrate my attempts so that I may be left with no recourse but you, the source of eternal life in Jesus. *Amen.*

"Come, Let Us Return"

Read Hosea 5:15–6:3

"Come, let us return to the Lord; for it is
  he who has torn, and he will heal us;
  he has struck down, and he will bind
  us up."

Hosea 6:1

God's intent is that his people will realize that he
is their only hope—that their distress will drive
them to his healing arms. These verses are a re-
markable anticipation of the healing for all men
and women that is accomplished in the resurrection of Jesus Christ.

Compare this with Luke 15:17–18. Is it the
same message?

PRAYER: Father in heaven, how merciful and compassionate you are! What an endless source of forgiveness and healing! I return to you again and
again from my feckless wandering and find myself
"ransomed, healed, restored, forgiven" (Henry
Francis Lyte, "Praise, My Soul, the King of Heaven,"
The Hymnbook, 31). Receive my praise in Jesus' name.
Amen.

AUGUST 23

"Not Sacrifice"

Read Hosea 6:4–7

For I desire steadfast love and not sacrifice,
the knowledge of God rather than burnt
offerings.

Hosea 6:6

It is a lot easier to *do* a religious act than to *be* a righteous person. And we keep trying to get by the easy way. But God won't let us: his prophetic word is insistent and unrelenting, calling us to "steadfast love" and the "knowledge of God."

Do you ever substitute a religious performance for an act of understanding or love? How do you do it?

PRAYER: If "the wild animals on all the mountains" (Psalm 50:10) are yours, O God, you certainly have no need of what I have. But you do seem to need what I can be in love and understanding to others. Today I will share that with friend and enemy as an offering to you, for Jesus' sake. *Amen.*

"They Murder"

Read Hosea 6:8–11

As robbers lie in wait for someone, so the
priests are banded together; they murder
on the road to Shechem, they commit a
monstrous crime.

Hosea 6:9

Shechem was the site of a famous church (place
of worship) in Hosea's time. Formal religion and
daily life were so far divorced that the very priests
who led in worship were plotting against the lives
of the worshipers.

Have you ever worshiped with someone (say a
brother, sister, husband, wife, neighbor) and at
the same time plotted some revenge against that
person?

PRAYER: I wonder how many times, Lord, I have
sat in church professing to love you and, "if looks
could kill," murdered someone in the next pew.
Help me to get my two loves, my love for you and
my love for my neighbor, together; through the
power of Jesus Christ. *Amen.*

"Their Deeds Surround Them"

Read Hosea 7:1–3

But they do not consider that I remember
all their wickedness. Now their deeds
surround them, they are before my face.

Hosea 7:2

We describe people who live thoughtlessly, without looking up to see where they are going, as "painting themselves into a corner." There comes a time when they can go no farther and are trapped—not by an enemy, but by what they themselves have done.

Can you recall an incident when you were "trapped" in your own sin?

PRAYER: O God, you are both my judge and my savior: show me the utter futility of persisting in my own ways, so I can freely throw myself on your mercy, in the name of Jesus. *Amen.*

"Like a Heated Oven"
Read Hosea 7:4–7

> They are all adulterers; they are like a
>   heated oven, whose baker does not
>   need to stir the fire, from the kneading
>   of the dough until it is leavened.

Hosea 7:4

The kings, who should have encouraged justice, instead delighted in evil. What they didn't reckon on was the evil backfiring on them. (Four kings were assassinated in twelve years during this period.) They were like bakers who fired up their ovens and then found that they had done their work too well, "finishing" themselves as well as what they put in the oven.

Can you think of anything similar in American history?

PRAYER: This message is plain enough, Lord. There is no way to hurt another without hurting myself. I want to put my energies in the other direction, conspiring to love and scheming for justice. *Amen.*

"A Cake Not Turned"

Read Hosea 7:8–10

Ephraim mixes himself with the peoples;
　Ephraim is a cake not turned.

Hosea 7:8

"Ephraim," another name for "Israel," refuses to let God finish his job with her. Far from mature, she still insists on rushing out and taking her place in the world. She needs to return to God and let him finish what he has begun. As it is, she is "half-baked."

In what ways are you immature?

PRAYER: O God, when I run here and there, frantically trying to find happiness and fulfillment, help me instead to wait before you and let you complete your good work in me, in Jesus Christ. *Amen.*

"Silly and Without Sense"
Read Hosea 7:11–13

Ephraim has become like a dove, silly and
    without sense; they call upon Egypt,
    they go to Assyria.

Hosea 7:11

Egypt and Assyria were the two world powers in
Hosea's day. He saw his nation fluttering back and
forth between them, perching for a while on one
side, and then on the other, silly and fickle as a
dove. His nation should have been trying to find
out what it meant to be God's people, not Egypt's
or Assyria's.

Describe a recent instance of your own indeci-
siveness.

PRAYER: Almighty God, you are faithful and constant in your love for me, and I'm faithless and
inconstant. Forgive me for my wavering and wandering. Grant me perseverance to stick to your
way revealed in Jesus. *Amen.*

"A Defective Bow"

Read Hosea 7:14–16

They turn to that which does not profit;
    they have become like a defective bow;
    their officials shall fall by the sword
    because of the rage of their tongue. So
    much for their babbling in the land of
    Egypt.

Hosea 7:16

A "defective bow" is one that is warped so that its arrows do not reach their target. The people are useless in the hands of their God. He has an "aim" for them, but they miss the mark.

What is the target toward which God is aiming you?

PRAYER: "Take Thou our minds, dear Lord, we humbly pray; Give us the mind of Christ each passing day; Teach us to know the truth that sets us free; Grant us in all our thoughts to honor Thee" (William Hiram Foulkes, "Take Thou Our Minds, Dear Lord," The Hymnbook, 306). Amen.

"Set the Trumpet"

Read Hosea 8:1–3

Set the trumpet to your lips! One like a
vulture is over the house of the Lord,
because they have broken my covenant,
and transgressed my law.

Hosea 8:1

The times are desperate! Do the people know it?
Or do they assume well-being? They only need to
look upward—there is a vulture hovering over the
dead and rotting corpse of Israel's religion. Blow
the warning trumpet!

Compare this with Romans 13:11–14.

PRAYER: "Awake, my soul, and with the sun Thy
daily stage of duty run: Shake off dull sloth, and
joyful rise To pay thy morning sacrifice" (Thomas
Ken, "Awake, My Soul, and with the Sun," *The
Hymnbook*, 50). In the name of Jesus. Amen.

"The Calf of Samaria"

Read Hosea 8:4–6

For it is from Israel, an artisan made it;
   it is not God. The calf of Samaria shall
   be broken to pieces.

Hosea 8:6

The Israelites had a vigorous religious business going—and not an atheist in the bunch! But their religion consisted of making gold-calf idols. It was a far cry from serving a living God.

Are you ever religious in a way that contradicts God's purposes for you?

PRAYER: Dear God, what a lot of time I waste doing religious things instead of, by faith, letting you work your way in me. Save me from idol-making, however subtle its forms, so that I can give my full attention to serving you, the living God revealed to me in Jesus Christ. *Amen.*

"Reap the Whirlwind"
Read Hosea 8:7–10

For they sow the wind, and they shall reap
the whirlwind. The standing grain has no
heads, it shall yield no meal; if it were to
yield, foreigners would devour it.

Hosea 8:7

The program was that Israel would sow seeds of justice that would reap a harvest of righteousness. But they sowed the wind—self-indulgent fantasies and words without actions (or, as we might say, "hot air"). The result would be, not a harvest of fruit, but a greater emptiness than ever—a whirlwind that would sweep the place clean.

What seeds (deeds) of faith are you planting that you believe will bear good fruit?

PRAYER: As you, O Lord, have faithfully sown the good seed of your word in the soil of my life, so may I continue that work of gospel planting and watering, while you give the growth through your Holy Spirit. Amen.

"Altars for Sinning"
Read Hosea 8:11–14

When Ephraim multiplied altars to expiate
sin, they became to him altars for sinning.
Hosea 8:11

The final irony was that the altars, which were built
to deal with sin, became places to sin; instead of
bringing human beings humbly to God, they became extravagant and pretentious exhibits of pride.

Does what you do in church get between you
and God?

PRAYER: "Investigate my life, O God, find out
everything about me; Cross-examine and test me,
get a clear picture of what I'm about; See for
yourself whether I've done anything wrong—
then guide me on the road to eternal life" (Psalm
139:23–24). *Amen.*

"Do Not Rejoice!"

Read Hosea 9:1–3

Do not rejoice, O Israel! Do not exult as
other nations do; for you have played
the whore, departing from your God.
You have loved a prostitute's pay on all
threshing floors.

Hosea 9:1

The scene is the autumn harvest festival—a time
of great rejoicing. But Hosea throws cold water on
the festivities: the people have been sacrificing to
pagan gods all year; they can't remedy that just by
"throwing a party" for God. A holiday celebration
is a poor substitute for a daily faith.

Do you save thoughts of God for special occa-
sions?

PRAYER: Lord, I want to share your joy every day.
By your Holy Spirit release a deep sense of well-
being within me that lets me participate hourly in
the joys of salvation, in Jesus Christ. *Amen.*

SEPTEMBER 4

"Mourners' Bread"

Read Hosea 9:4

They shall not pour drink offerings of wine
to the Lord, and their sacrifices shall not
please him. Such sacrifices shall be like
mourners' bread; all who eat of it shall
be defiled; for their bread shall be for
their hunger only; it shall not come to
the house of the Lord.

Hosea 9:4

"Mourners' bread," bread eaten in the house of
one who is dead, makes people by Hebrew law
"unclean" and ineligible to come to the temple
(Numbers 19:11). The people are about to go to
the homelands (Egypt and Assyria) of gods with
which they are enamored—dead gods—and have
their meals there. How much rejoicing will there
be at *that* party?

What are some things that defile instead of en-
hance your life?

PRAYER: I am determined, O God, to sustain my
life on your word and no other. Use your "bread
of life" to build a healthy spirit in me that knows
how to worship and serve in Jesus' name. *Amen.*

"Egypt Shall Gather Them"
Read Hosea 9:5–6

> For even if they escape destruction, Egypt
> shall gather them, Memphis shall bury
> them. Nettles shall possess their precious
> things of silver; thorns shall be in their
> tents.
>
> Hosea 9:6

The Feast of Tabernacles was also called the Feast
of Ingathering, referring to the gathering in of the
autumn harvest. The prophet sees a different kind
of harvest gathering in the future: the seeds sown
in disobedience will result, not in festival, but in
his people being gathered into the famous but
weed-covered graveyards of Egypt.

If Hosea could examine your daily life, do you
think he would have any warnings to give? What
might they be?

PRAYER: O God, by your prophets you expose the
seriousness of my sin, and in Jesus you demonstrate the power of forgiveness: grant me a ready
heart to receive your gift of life, in Jesus' name.
Amen.

"The Prophet Is a Fool"

Read Hosea 9:7–9

The days of punishment have come, the
days of recompense have come; Israel
cries, "The prophet is a fool, the man of
the spirit is mad!" Because of your
iniquity, your hostility is great.

Hosea 9:7

This is the only clue in Hosea as to how his com-
patriots thought of him. The passage is tantaliz-
ingly brief but clear enough to let us see that they
treated him with scorn and contempt. They classi-
fied him ("man of the spirit") in order to dismiss
him ("is mad").

Has your Christian witness ever caused you to
be derided by others?

PRAYER: I want, O God, to be shaped by your word
and spirit, not by the opinions or expectations of
others; and if that means being considered a fool,
help me to remember that the "foolishness of God
is wiser than men," in Jesus' name. Amen.

"Became Detestable"
Read Hosea 9:10–14

Like grapes in the wilderness, I found
    Israel. Like the first fruit on the fig tree,
in its first season, I saw your ancestors.
But they came to Baal-peor, and con-
    secrated themselves to a thing of shame,
and became detestable like the thing
    they loved.

Hosea 9:10

With nostalgia God recalls the good days of the
people's life in the wilderness before they came to
Baal-peor, the outpost of Canaanite religion where
they indulged in the fertility rites of the corrupt
god Baal. And now the final irony: worship at the
fertility shrines has produced infertility.

Read the story of Baal-peor in Numbers 25:1–5.

PRAYER: Grant, gracious God, that I may be among
those who "are being changed into his likeness
from one degree of glory to another" (2 Corinthians 3:19) through the working of your Spirit.
Amen.

"Gilgal"

Read Hosea 9:15–17

Every evil of theirs began at Gilgal; there
    I came to hate them. Because of the
    wickedness of their deeds I will drive
    them out of my house. I will love them
    no more; all their officials are rebels.

Hosea 9:15

Israelites pointed back with pride to Gilgal, where
Saul's kingship was inaugurated (1 Samuel 11).
Hosea looks back at it and says, "That is where the
trouble started, for there you started looking to
men instead of God for leadership."

    Do you ever confuse loyalty to government with
obedience to God?

PRAYER: "Tie in a living tether The prince and
priest and thrall; Bind all our lives together, Smite
us and save us all; In ire and exultation Aflame
with faith, and free, Lift up a living nation, A single sword to Thee" (G. K. Chesterton, "O God of
Earth and Altar," *The Hymnbook*, 511). For Jesus'
sake. *Amen.*

"Their Heart Is False"

Read Hosea 10:1–2

Their heart is false; now they must bear
their guilt. The Lord will break down
their altars, and destroy their pillars.

Hosea 10:2

As they prospered, the people greedily built more altars and pillars to make sure they would be even more prosperous. They were using worship as a way of getting things from God instead of putting themselves at the mercy and service of God.

Is there a similarity between this and Jesus' story in Luke 12:16–21?

PRAYER: How false it would be of me, God, to increase my prayers if they consisted only of artful schemes to get you to pass out more blessings in my direction. In my prayers I want to cultivate a simple, grateful openness to your spirit, through Jesus. Amen.

"Like Poisonous Weeds"
Read Hosea 10:3–4

They utter mere words; with empty oaths
   they make covenants; so litigation springs
   up like poisonous weeds in the furrows
   of the field.

Hosea 10:4

God in his judgment is about to remove the kingship from Israel. But, says Hosea, it is no great
loss. What could kings do for them anyhow? They
broke their oaths continually, and their adminis-
tration of justice was so foul that it produced
nothing but a crop of poisonous weeds.

Whom do you trust more, God or government?

PRAYER: "O where are kings and empires now Of
old that went and came? But, Lord, Thy Church is
praying yet, A thousand years the same" (Arthur
Cleveland Coxe, "O Where Are Kings and Empires
Now," The Hymnbook, 431). Amen.

"The Calf of Beth-aven"
Read Hosea 10:5–6

The inhabitants of Samaria tremble for the
calf of Beth-aven. Its people shall mourn
for it, and its idolatrous priests shall wail
over it, over its glory that has departed
from it.

Hosea 10:5

During a time of danger when the enemy army is
about to invade and loot the country, the people
are crying over the imminent loss of the "god,"
the magnificent gold bull-calf set up in their place
of worship. And Hosea is full of scorn for their
silliness.

Do you have too small an idea of God?

PRAYER: Holy God, may I have the "power to comprehend with all the saints what is the breadth
and length and height and depth, and to know the
love of Christ which surpasses knowledge" (Ephesians 3:18–19). *Amen.*

"Cover Us"

Read Hosea 10:7–8

The high places of Aven, the sin of Israel,
shall be destroyed. Thorn and thistle
shall grow up on their altars. They shall
say to the mountains, Cover us, and to
the hills, Fall on us.

Hosea 10:8

As God clears away the accumulated corruption of
the age—king, bull-image, high places (local sites
of worship)—the people are going to feel "naked"
and cry out to the mountains to cover them. But
the mountains aren't going to do it. And the people
are going to find that they are exposed to the
purpose and mercy of God.

What are some of the things that get between
you and God?

PRAYER: O God, do whatever is necessary in my
life to keep me open to your presence. If it means
taking away things that I am too dependent upon
and removing things that interfere with your will,
I am ready for that, for Jesus' sake. *Amen.*

"The Days of Gibeah"
Read Hosea 10:9–10

Since the days of Gibeah you have sinned,
   O Israel; there they have continued. Shall
   not war overtake them in Gibeah?

Hosea 10:9

Hosea uses old events to interpret the present. Gibeah was the site of a wanton violation of morals, which had been swiftly punished (Judges 19–21). Since the style of sinning continues, the style of judgment will continue also.

What event in your past is useful still as a warning?

PRAYER: Help me, dear God, not to stupidly repeat old sins and have to suffer old judgments. Help me to grow, learning from both my sins and your grace, letting your salvation build me into a mature person, grown up in Christ. *Amen.*

"Break Up Your Fallow Ground"
Read Hosea 10:11–12

Sow for yourselves righteousness; reap
steadfast love; break up your fallow
ground; for it is time to seek the Lord,
that he may come and rain righteousness
upon you.

Hosea 10:12

The people have been lazily living off the heritage
of their ancestors. The easy work of threshing, ben-
efiting from what others have sown and reaped,
must now give way to the hard work of plowing
and harrowing. There is much work to do: righteousness to be sown and steadfast love to be har-
vested. It's time to get to work!

What is the most important thing you have to
do today?

PRAYER: O Father, when I remember the words of
your Son, "Take my yoke upon you and learn
from me . . . for my yoke is easy and my burden is
light," your commands do not seem onerous, but
pleasant. Thank you for good work to do and gracious commands to guide me. *Amen.*

"The Tumult of War"

Read Hosea 10:13–15

Therefore the tumult of war shall rise
against your people, and all your fortresses shall be destroyed, as Shalman
destroyed Beth-arbel on the day of battle
when mothers were dashed in pieces
with their children.

Hosea 10:14

The Israelites were trusting in military might so they wouldn't have to trust in God. Chariots and warriors were a substitute for faith. Their faith in God could have made them great among the nations; their faith in militarism would result in devastation.

Compare Matthew 26:51–52 with Hosea.

PRAYER: "Lord God of Hosts, whose purpose, never swerving, Leads toward the day of Jesus Christ Thy Son, Grant us to march among Thy faithful legions, Armed with Thy courage, till the world is won" (Shepherd Knapp, "Lord God of Hosts, Whose Purpose, Never Swerving," The Hymnbook, 288). Amen.

"When Israel Was a Child"

Read Hosea 11:1–2

When Israel was a child, I loved him,
and out of Egypt I called my son.

Hosea 11:1

The original relationship between God and Israel was love. The nation was created by love, a love that expressed itself by bringing the people out of Egypt in the exodus and making them a people free to worship and serve their God.

Have you ever loved someone and had that person spurn your love? How does it feel?

PRAYER: God of love, your word makes me what I am, defines my beginning and my end. May it also shape my present actions so that I may be a child who brings honor to your name through Jesus Christ. *Amen.*

"Bands of Love"

Read Hosea 11:3—4

I led them with cords of human kindness,
  with bands of love. I was to them like
  those who lift infants to their cheeks.
  I bent down to them and fed them.

Hosea 11:4

How could the people reject God when he, like a father, had held them by the hand while they made their first faltering steps, gathered them up in his arms when they fell, and healed their hurts?

What period of Israel's history corresponds to this infant and father imagery?

PRAYER: Dear God, you treat my immaturity with understanding and my trouble with compassion. But I do not want always to be a child: I want to become a mature disciple, even as you have called me to be in Jesus Christ. Amen.

"Does Not Raise Them"

Read Hosea 11:5–7

My people are bent on turning away from
me. To the Most High they call, but he
does not raise them up at all.

Hosea 11:7

Disregard for God's help is destroying the nation
and will soon return them to the slavery from
which God had saved them centuries earlier. In
contrast to the time of beginnings when Israel's
existence was the work of God's fatherly care, the
present is perilous and tragic.

What could Israel have done to avoid the pre-
dicted disaster?

PRAYER: O Christ, give me the understanding that
can hear these stern words of warning as part of
your plan of salvation, words to keep me from
folly and thoughtless wandering, so I can consis-
tently choose your yoke and not the yoke of another. *Amen.*

"I Am God and No Mortal"
Read Hosea 11:8–9

I will not execute my fierce anger; I will
   not again destroy Ephraim; for I am God
   and no mortal, the Holy One in your
   midst, and I will not come in wrath.

Hosea 11:9

It appears that we deserve rejection; but there is
something more powerfully at work, namely, divine compassion. God has redemptive ways of ex-
ecuting judgment: destruction is not his business;
salvation is.

Have you ever had (or been) a rebellious child?
Compare your feelings with those expressed by
God.

PRAYER: God of grace, how I praise you for working out my salvation, not angrily getting rid of
me. I know I am not now what I should be; make
me what you will me to be, through the power of
your Holy Spirit. *Amen.*

"Roars Like a Lion"
Read Hosea 11:10–12

They shall go after the Lord, who roars like
a lion; when he roars, his children shall
come trembling from the west.

Hosea 11:10

Salvation does not cancel judgment, but it changes
it from something horrible to be avoided to an
awesome reality to be believed. The lion's roar of
God, terrible and majestic, is a sign of hope for the
people: God is mightily at work and will accomplish his will.

Are you afraid of God?

PRAYER: Your call, Almighty God, is clear and urgent. May my response be direct and plain. I neither can nor would avoid your call. My answer is yes; I will be your child through Jesus Christ. Amen.

"Ephraim Herds the Wind"
Read Hosea 12:1

Ephraim herds the wind, and pursues the
    east wind all day long; they multiply
    falsehood and violence; they make a
    treaty with Assyria, and oil is carried to
    Egypt.

Hosea 12:1

The prophet sketches a cartoon: The people are
herdsmen to the wind. They are anxiously tend-
ing to something (Assyria and Egypt) completely
unpredictable—and acting as if they were serious
about it! They should be spending their energy on
something personal and real—namely, their God.

Is the most visible always the most real?

PRAYER: I wonder what Hosea would say to me,
Lord. What would he see in my life that is silly
and pretentious—things that have a look of solid
reality but in fact are foolish substitutes for the
great reality that is your presence and purpose in
me? Amen.

"Return to Your God"

Read Hosea 12:2–6

But as for you, return to your God,
    hold fast to love and justice, and
    wait continually for your God.

Hosea 12:6

Jacob had a bad start, and he compounded it with a life of treachery. But he struggled with God and finally arrived at a life of faith, love, and justice. The present generation can do it, too. An unsavory history disqualifies nobody.

What part of the Jacob story do you like best?

PRAYER: You don't give up on me, God; why should I give up? As often as I depart from your word, I will return for forgiveness. Receive me in mercy. Continue to call and command me in Jesus' name. *Amen.*

"False Balances"

Read Hosea 12:7–9

A trader, in whose hands are false balances,
   he loves to oppress.

Hosea 12:7

Israel was bragging about its wealth, assuming, as many do, that wealth is a sign of divine blessing. The prophet sees behind the boast to the actual reason for their riches: they are a bunch of cheaters— they have rigged the scales!

What punishment does God announce? Do you think it is appropriate?

PRAYER: "Put false ways far from me; and graciously teach me your law. I have chosen the way of faithfulness; I set your ordinances before me. I cling to your decrees, O Lord; let me not be put to shame. I run the way of your commandments, for you enlarge my understanding" (Psalm 119:29–32). Amen.

"By a Prophet"

Read Hosea 12:10–14

By a prophet the Lord brought Israel up
from Egypt, and by a prophet he was
guarded.

Hosea 12:13

The prophets, those unusual men and women
who perceived God's action and heard God's
word and then bravely told the people what they
had seen and heard, are at the center of biblical religion; not the complicated arrangements for sacrifice, which degenerated into a manipulation of
feelings and a cover for selfishness.

Who are your favorite prophets?

PRAYER: "God of the prophets! Bless the prophets'
sons; Elijah's mantle o'er Elisha cast; Each age its
solemn task may claim but once; Make each one
nobler, stronger than the last" (Denis Wortman,
"God of the Prophets!" *The Hymnbook,* 520). *Amen.*

"People Are Kissing Calves!"
Read Hosea 13:1–3

And now they keep on sinning and make a cast image for themselves, idols of silver made according to their understanding, all of them the work of artisans. "Sacrifice to these," they say. People are kissing calves!

Hosea 13:2

Worship makes a person better than he or she was—or worse. Worship of the living God builds strength and vitality in us; worship of an idol empties us of meaning and substance so we become hollow and trivial.

Read what Jesus said about worship in John 4:23–24.

PRAYER: Things keep crowding themselves into my field of worship—objects of beauty, items of desire—and threaten to push you, O God, out of the center. Stay at the center of my life. In my worship I will reaffirm your presence and believe in your salvation through Jesus. Amen.

SEPTEMBER 26

"A Bear Robbed of Her Cubs"
Read Hosea 13:4–11

I will fall upon them like a bear robbed of
her cubs, and will tear open the cover-
ing of their heart; there I will devour
them like a lion, as a wild animal would
mangle them.

Hosea 13:8

That men and women should forget the God who
saved and nourished them is not a matter that God
treats with indifference. He cares deeply enough
about us to be angry when we depart from his
loving purpose for us.

If you had to make a choice, which would you
prefer: God angry with you or God indifferent to
you?

PRAYER: I know, dear God, how much you care
about what I am and what I do. Be with me, even
if it means that I must experience your anger, so
that I may neither wander nor drift, but live with
joyful hope in Jesus. *Amen.*

"An Unwise Son"

Read Hosea 13:12–13

The pangs of childbirth come for him, but
he is an unwise son; for at the proper
time he does not present himself at the
mouth of the womb.

Hosea 13:13

A startling illustration: A people is conceived, de-
velops in the womb, and is ready to be born. Then
(impossibly it seems), the infant refuses to enter
the world. The infant is Israel, insisting on the
half-life of an embryo, a shadow life in the womb,
when God wants her to live openly in faith in the
wide world of his creation.

Do you see a similarity between this and John
3:1–5?

PRAYER: Bring to birth, Creator Spirit, the seeds of
righteousness and new life you have sown in me.
Make me in the image of him who shows forth
your will and redemption, even Jesus Christ my
Lord. Amen.

"O Death, Where Are Your Plagues?"
Read Hosea 13:14

Shall I ransom them from the power of
    Sheol? Shall I redeem them from Death?
O Death, where are your plagues?
O Sheol, where is your destruction?
Compassion is hidden from my eyes.

Hosea 13:14

Things couldn't be worse: God's people have com-
piled a history of sin that is overwhelming. Judgment is necessary and destruction inevitable. But
God interrupts death. "Ransom" and "redeem" are
better by far (and more powerful!) than "death."

Note how Paul quotes this verse in 1 Corinthians 15:55.

PRAYER: Thank you, great God: you break the
cause-and-effect chain of sin and death in me;
you surprise me with gospel and promises. Thank
you, O thank you, God of resurrection! *Amen.*

"A Blast from the Lord"

Read Hosea 13:15–16

Although he may flourish among rushes,
    the east wind shall come, a blast from
    the Lord, rising from the wilderness;
    and his fountain shall dry up, his spring
    shall be parched. It shall strip his trea-
    sury of every precious thing.

Hosea 13:15

Humankind cannot hope to salvage anything from its sin. God will wipe out both the sin and its so-called benefits in much the same way as the dread east wind comes out of the desert and dries up everything in its path.

Why is judgment necessary?

PRAYER: Father, I would much rather listen to your promise of salvation and future bliss than these warnings of judgment. But like it or not, they are here. Use them to keep me alert and honest with you, O God, in Jesus' name. *Amen.*

"The Orphan Finds Mercy"
Read Hosea 14:1–3

Assyria shall not save us; we will not ride
   upon horses; we will say no more, "Our
   God," to the work of our hands. In you
   the orphan finds mercy.

Hosea 14:3

No judgment is inevitable. Repentance can radically change the course of events. The moment we turn away from all god-substitutes—become an "orphan" to the world—and return to God, new life begins to flow.

Which phrase here is appropriate as a "key verse" to summarize Hosea?

PRAYER: The power of your word to me, O Christ, batters all resistance, penetrates all defense. Mercy overtakes judgment, and I know you not as my punisher but as my savior. Praise God! *Amen.*

"I Will Heal Their Disloyalty"
Read Hosea 14:4–7

I will heal their disloyalty; I will love them
freely, for my anger has turned from
them.

Hosea 14:4

Hosea's message builds to a gospel climax: the love
of God moving on a pivot of forgiveness over-
comes all rebellion and iniquity. The metaphors of
judgment—dry and barren—give way to a lush,
Eden-like flourishing of peace and righteousness.

Can you think of anything in Jesus' ministry
that sounds similar to this?

PRAYER: God, as you move in me in great mercy, I
am conscious of your healing and your peace. As
your blessing abounds, my praise builds, in the
name of Father, Son, and Holy Spirit. *Amen.*

OCTOBER 2

"Those Who Are Wise"
Read Hosea 14:8–9

Those who are wise understand these
things; those who are discerning know
them. For the ways of the Lord are right,
and the upright walk in them, but trans-
gressors stumble in them.

Hosea 14:9

A last word: In the light of such persistent love,
who can or would resist? Knowing the intensity
of God's love for us and his disgust for all idols,
who could prefer the idol to the Savior?

What do you like best about Hosea?

PRAYER: "Your love, Yahweh, fills the earth! Train
me to live by your counsel. Be good to your servant, Yahweh; be as good as your Word. Train
me in good common sense; I'm thoroughly committed to living your way. Before I learned to answer you, I wandered all over the place, but now
I'm in step with your Word. You are good, and
the source of good; train me in your goodness"
(Psalm 119:57–60). *Amen.*

"The Words of Amos"

Read Amos 1:1

> The words of Amos, who was among
> the shepherds of Tekoa, which he saw
> concerning Israel in the days of King
> Uzziah of Judah and in the days of King
> Jeroboam son of Joash of Israel, two
> years before the earthquake.
>
> *Amos 1:1*

Amos is the first in the succession of prophets whose preaching is preserved in writing. What he preached to Israel in the eighth century B.C. continues to be used by the Holy Spirit to attack our conscience and stir our hearts to obedience.

What do you know of Amos?

PRAYER: God of the prophets, use the words of your prophet Amos to speak your eternal word to me, to make me aware of my sin and your righteousness, to expose my inclinations to disobedience and illuminate your abundant mercy, in the name and for the sake of Jesus Christ. *Amen.*

OCTOBER 4

"The Lord Roars"

Read Amos 1:2

And he said: The Lord roars from Zion,
  and utters his voice from Jerusalem;
  the pastures of the shepherds wither,
  and the top of Carmel dries up.

Amos 1:2

There is nothing timid or bashful about Amos: his is no gently insinuated message. His words are a yell, shattering complacency. One of the effects of sin is to dull our spiritual senses and lull us into self-indulgent sloth: the prophet wakes us up to God.

Do you ever go to sleep in church?

PRAYER: Never, Lord, let me suppose that the gospel message is soothing background music to my life: I want to hear the roar of your commands, the crashing cadences of your earthshaking, life-changing words, even in Jesus Christ. *Amen.*

"Transgressions of Damascus"
Read Amos 1:3–5

> Thus says the Lord: For three transgressions
> of Damascus, and for four, I will not
> revoke the punishment; because they
> have threshed Gilead with threshing
> sledges of iron.
>
> *Amos 1:3*

A series of eight "punishment sayings," of which
this is the first, begins at the outside perimeter of
Israel's concern (Damascus) and moves steadily
inward to finally face the Israelites with the consequences of their own sins (2:6ff.). Amos's strategy is clear: he will use an awareness of others'
sins to develop a realization of personal sins.

Whose sins bother you the most?

PRAYER: God of love and justice, as I become aware
of the enormity of the crimes against humanity
that take place in other nations, help me to realize
my own waywardness and rebellion so that I may
be led to true repentance in Jesus Christ. *Amen.*

OCTOBER 6

"Transgressions of Gaza"
Read Amos 1:6–8

Thus says the Lord: For three transgressions
of Gaza, and for four, I will not revoke
the punishment; because they carried
into exile entire communities, to hand
them over to Edom.

Amos 1:6

Gaza, Ashdod, Ashkelon, and Ekron were the
chief cities of the Philistines, archenemies of Israel. The Philistines, knowing no language but
that of the sword, were a constant harassment to
those who were learning to live by faith.

What story of the Philistines is most familiar
to you?

PRAYER: God, in my daily encounter with minds
brutalized by ambition and with spirits sluggish
with self-indulgence, help me not to be overcome
by evil but to overcome evil with good, in Jesus'
name. *Amen.*

"Transgressions of Tyre"

Read Amos 1:9–10

> Thus says the Lord: For three transgressions
> of Tyre, and for four, I will not revoke
> the punishment; because they delivered
> entire communities over to Edom, and
> did not remember the covenant of
> kinship.

Amos 1:9

The failure to keep one's word both betrays truth and dissolves society into a jungle. The failure to "remember the covenant of kinship" reduces humanity to bestiality. It happens often in human affairs, but it is no less horrible for its frequency.

Where was Tyre?

PRAYER: God, you have made peoples to live together in peace and justice. Grant that all may learn your ways, and find ways to establish bonds of trust and not betray them. In the name of Jesus, Lord of the nations. *Amen.*

OCTOBER 8

"Transgressions of Edom"
Read Amos 1:11–12

Thus says the Lord: For three transgressions
of Edom, and for four, I will not revoke
the punishment; because he pursued his
brother with the sword and cast off all
pity; he maintained his anger perpetu-
ally, and kept his wrath forever.

Amos 1:11

Anger is the theme of Edom's sin—the wild, relentless energy that is against another and not for
him or her, that destroys and does not create, that
tears down and does not build up.

Where was Edom?

PRAYER: "O God of earth and altar, Bow down and
hear our cry; Our earthly rulers falter, Our people
drift and die; The walls of gold entomb us, The
swords of scorn divide; Take not Thy thunder from
us, But take away our pride" (G. K. Chesterton, "O
God of Earth and Altar," *The Hymnbook*, 511). *Amen.*

"Transgressions of the Ammonites"
Read Amos 1:13–15

Thus says the Lord: For three transgressions
of the Ammonites, and for four, I will
not revoke the punishment; because they
have ripped open pregnant women in
Gilead in order to enlarge their territory.

Amos 1:13

Ambitious greed—"in order to enlarge their territory"—is a recurrent theme in the human story. It is put forth as a permissible excuse for the most terrible outrages. The biblical mind, though, judges actions not by their material success but by their personal consequences. Not things, but people, are the concern.

Where was Ammon?

PRAYER: "From all that terror teaches, From lies of tongue and pen; From all the easy speeches That comfort cruel men; From sale and profanation Of honor and the sword; From sleep and from damnation, Deliver us, good Lord!" (G. K. Chesterton, "O God of Earth and Altar," *The Hymnbook*, 511). *Amen.*

"Transgressions of Moab"
Read Amos 2:1–3

Thus says the Lord: For three transgressions
of Moab, and for four, I will not revoke
the punishment; because he burned to
lime the bones of the king of Edom.

Amos 2:1

Evil destroys an embryo (1:13) with the same
ruthlessness with which it desecrates a corpse
(2:1). Nothing is exempted from its rapacious-
ness. The elimination of God from life is a first
step in the dehumanization of men and women.
Denial of God's majesty very quickly produces a
society of indignities and atrocities.

Where was Moab?

PRAYER: "Tie in a living tether The prince and
priest and thrall; Bind all our lives together, Smite
us and save us all; In ire and exultation Aflame
with faith, and free, Lift up a living nation, A single sword to Thee" (G. K. Chesterton, "O God of
Earth and Altar," *The Hymnbook,* 511). *Amen.*

"Transgressions of Judah"

Read Amos 2:4–5

> Thus says the Lord: For three transgressions
> of Judah, and for four, I will not revoke
> the punishment; because they have
> rejected the law of the Lord, and have
> not kept his statutes, but they have been
> led astray by the same lies after which
> their ancestors walked.

Amos 2:4

This people who were heirs to a magnificent revelation of God and who had experienced a merciful salvation by God had, nevertheless, chosen to abandon the revelation and exchange the experience for cheap lies.

What are some of the lies that America lives by?

PRAYER: Eternal God, help me always to prefer the hard truth that gives my life eternity and wholeness, and always to reject the easy lies that promise much but fulfill little. In the name of Jesus. Amen.

"Transgressions of Israel"

Read Amos 2:6–8

Thus says the Lord: For three transgressions
of Israel, and for four, I will not revoke
the punishment; because they sell the
righteous for silver, and the needy for a
pair of sandals.

Amos 2:6

In a series of seven "punishment sayings" Amos
has aroused the indignation of Israel against the
sins of her neighbors; now in this eighth repetition of the formula, he directs it to herself. Will
Israel, who is up in arms at the evil in others, be
as hard on herself?

Are you as quick to discover sins in yourself as
in others?

PRAYER: God, use my capacity for righteous indignation, which I practice so freely among others,
to convict myself so that no cruelties may be committed unawares and no hurtful words spoken
unknowingly. For Jesus' sake. *Amen.*

"I Brought You Up"

Read Amos 2:9–10

Also I brought you up out of the land of
Egypt, and led you forty years in the
wilderness, to possess the land of the
Amorite.

Amos 2:10

Israel did not get the land on which they were now
living on their own. God got it for them by dis-
posing of the Amorites, who had stood between
them and the conquest of Canaan. But Israel, instead of living in gratitude, dishonored the gift of
land with their careless morals.

How do you show your gratitude for the free
life God gives you?

PRAYER: God, all I am and all I have was bought
with a price. I don't want to take any of it for
granted but live in ways that express my joy in
your will, in Jesus Christ. *Amen.*

"Some of Your Children"

Read Amos 2:11–12

And I raised up some of your children to
be prophets and some of your youths
to be Nazirites. Is it not indeed so,
O people of Israel? says the Lord.

Amos 2:11

God honored Israel by choosing some from her
number to speak the word of God (prophets) and
others from her number to show the ways of God
(Nazirites). Israel, though, in her headlong plunge
into a life of self-indulgence, made a mockery of
the high offices.

Who were some of the prophets God raised up?

PRAYER: Holy God, forgive me when I fail to recognize and honor your servants, the men and
women who have been singled out for special
callings. Use them to speak your word to me and
show your ways to me. *Amen.*

"Flight Shall Perish from the Swift"

Read Amos 2:13–16

Flight shall perish from the swift, and the
strong shall not retain their strength, nor
shall the mighty save their lives.

Amos 2:14

Worldly prosperity is no defense against God's justice. Despite her privilege, despite her blessings, despite her gifts, Israel will be punished. God's righteousness will not be flouted.

Why was Israel about to be punished?

PRAYER: Father, help me to use whatever strengths I have as tools for doing your will, not as a means to indulge myself. Give me a sensitive conscience and a compassionate heart, for Jesus' sake. *Amen.*

OCTOBER 16

"You Only Have I Known"

Read Amos 3:1–2

You only have I known of all the families of
the earth; therefore I will punish you for
all your iniquities.

Amos 3:2

The people had mistaken "chosen" for "pampered." Instead of becoming faithful sons and
daughters, quick to respond in gratitude and share
in love, they had become spoiled children.

For what kind of life has God chosen you?

PRAYER: What an immense privilege, Lord, to
know your name, to experience your love, to be
led in your ways. Thank you for your revelation;
guide me to live in its light, through Jesus Christ.
Amen.

"The Lion Has Roared"

Read Amos 3:3–8

The lion has roared; who will not fear?
The Lord God has spoken; who can but
prophesy?

Amos 3:8

Nine questions, drawn from everyday observations, train the mind to think in terms of cause and effect. The prophetic word of judgment is not a random accident; and it is not the figment of a gloomy imagination; it is *caused*—God has spoken.

How is this similar to 2 Corinthians 4:18?

PRAYER: Help me to see the hidden, secret cause of all things in you, O God; to be aware of and responsive to the reality of the unseen world where you will, where your love originates and now impinges on my daily life. *Amen.*

OCTOBER 18

"Oppressions"

Read Amos 3:9

Proclaim to the strongholds in Ashdod, and
  to the strongholds in the land of Egypt,
  and say, "Assemble yourselves on Mount
  Samaria, and see what great tumults are
  within it, and what oppressions are in its
  midst."

Amos 3:9

An invitation goes out to leaders in Assyria and
Egypt, who are specialists in the art of oppression,
to take a look at what is going on under the
Samaritan mountains. Even they, hardened and
calloused as they are to scenes of violence, will be
surprised at what they see in Israel.

What evil acts in our culture have you become
so used to that you no longer "see" them?

PRAYER: God, I live in the midst of violence without batting an eye. I have learned to take wickedness in my stride. Make me aware of the difference between right and wrong so that I may, with
all my heart, do battle for the right, in Jesus' name.
Amen.

"Robbery in Their Strongholds"
Read Amos 3:10–11

They do not know how to do right, says
the Lord, those who store up violence
and robbery in their strongholds.

Amos 3:10

The word "strongholds" gets special attention in
Amos. It is an architectural term describing the
residences of the wealthy and ruling urban classes.
But what is inside these expressions of developed
culture? Not the flowering of culture and morals
that we might expect, but the most barbaric forms
of violence.

What is behind the walls of your house?

PRAYER: Almighty God, grant that I may never
equate prosperity with righteousness, or take my
orders from the rich, or copy my morals from the
powerful, but always look to you for the word
that will command and bless me. *Amen.*

"A Piece of an Ear"

Read Amos 3:12

Thus says the Lord: As the shepherd
    rescues from the mouth of the lion
    two legs, or a piece of an ear, so shall
    the people of Israel who live in Samaria
    be rescued, with the corner of a couch
    and part of a bed.

Amos 3:12

An old legal custom lies behind this saying: if an animal was plundered from the flock, the shepherd had to show what was left of the carcass to its owner as proof that he had not stolen or sold the animal (Exodus 22:13). And that is all that will be left of Israel—evidence of the judgment.

Compare this with Amos 6:4–7.

PRAYER: I look for loopholes and escape clauses in your word, God, trying to avoid facing up to your love and judgment. Bring me back to the place of confession, repentance, and faith, through Jesus Christ my Lord. *Amen.*

"The Houses of Ivory"
Read *Amos* 3:13–15

I will tear down the winter house as well as
the summer house; and the houses of
ivory shall perish, and the great houses
shall come to an end, says the Lord.

Amos 3:15

"House" is the key word in this saying. Houses for
worship (beth-el) and houses for residence that are
built on crimes against the poor will be destroyed.
Magnificent structures that are constructed on
mean foundations will fall to the ground.

Compare this with Jesus' saying in Matthew
7:24–27.

PRAYER: Dear Jesus, I want the church where I
worship and the house in which I live to be places
for love, where my love for you is deepened and
my love for others shared. *Amen.*

"You Cows of Bashan"

Read *Amos* 4:1

> Hear this word, you cows of Bashan who
> are on Mount Samaria, who oppress the
> poor, who crush the needy, who say to
> their husbands, "Bring something to
> drink!"

Amos 4:1

The upper-class women in Samaria are a spoiled, petulant lot whose luxury is paid for by crushing the poor. When one person's ease is purchased at the price of another person's suffering, the prophet cries "Sin!"

Are there American parallels to what Amos saw in Samaria?

PRAYER: God, show me the behind-the-scenes realities in my world—what goes on with the down-and-out, what happens to the poor. I would be indifferent to no person's suffering, for Jesus' sake. *Amen.*

"Take You Away with Hooks"
Read Amos 4:2–3

The Lord God has sworn by his holiness:
> The time is surely coming upon you,
> when they shall take you away with
> hooks, even the last of you with
> fishhooks.

Amos 4:2

Hooks in the nose are used to lead stupid cattle who will not respond to verbal commands. When a people show no evidence of being able to respond to God's words of love and justice, and insensitively trample the lives of others in the mud, they also will be led away to where they cannot endanger the community.

Are you a careful listener to God's word?

PRAYER: You have given me ears to hear, O God. Train me in careful listening. Help me to hear all that you are saying to me in your scriptures and to respond in faith, in and through Jesus Christ. Amen.

"Come to Bethel . . . to Gilgal"

Read Amos 4:4–5

Come to Bethel—and transgress; to
   Gilgal—and multiply transgression;
   bring your sacrifices every morning,
   your tithes every three days.

Amos 4:4

Bethel and Gilgal were the two most important places for worship in Israel. Amos parodies the people's practices there: their pieties are blatant cover-ups for deliberate sins; the smoke from the sacrificial animals is a smoke screen for unrepentant wickedness. The worst sins, still, take place in church.

What happens when you worship?

PRAYER: Save me, Lord, from any act in church or out of it that separates me from your presence, or diverts me from loving, or becomes a substitute for being compassionate. *Amen.*

"Yet You Did Not Return"

Read Amos 4:6–8

I gave you cleanness of teeth in all your
    cities, and lack of bread in all your
    places, yet you did not return to me,
    says the Lord.

Amos 4:6

What does it take to wake this people up? What
does it take to bring them to their knees, reveren-
tially aware of God's glorious will among them?
Famine and drought were, it seemed, ineffective.
What does it take?

    Why did Israel not return?

PRAYER: God, I would be responsive to your chastening hand. Train me up in the ways that I should
go and let me not, ever, depart from the way of
your holiness, where your blessings flow. *Amen.*

"Blight and Mildew"

Read Amos 4:9–10

I struck you with blight and mildew; I laid
waste your gardens and your vineyards;
the locust devoured your fig trees and
your olive trees; yet you did not return
to me, says the Lord.

Amos 4:9

Crop failure and military defeat are likewise ineffective in shaking the people out of their sinful
ways. The people are thick-skinned: habituated in
selfishness, they are indifferent to the disciplining
rod that God uses to bring them into a fellowship
of love.

How does God discipline you?

PRAYER: Father, I know that you discipline those
whom you love and chastise those whom you
cherish: I welcome your judgments and receive
your corrections as you guide me in righteousness, even through Jesus Christ. *Amen.*

"Snatched from the Fire"

Read Amos 4:11

I overthrew some of you, as when God
overthrew Sodom and Gomorrah, and
you were like a brand snatched from the
fire; yet you did not return to me, says
the Lord.

Amos 4:11

Out of a raging fire that is consuming everything
and everyone and from which nothing can escape, God snatches Israel to salvation. Her very
existence can be traced to that miraculous rescue,
yet she lives forgetful and unrepentant.

How were you saved?

PRAYER: Help me, God, to realize the sheer mira-
cle of my life—the absolute and fantastic incredi-
bility of my very being. Realizing it helps me to
live in the deepest gratitude to you for saving me
from destruction, for putting the ground beneath
me and the heavens above me, so that I may live
by your grace in praise. *Amen.*

"Prepare to Meet Your God"

Read Amos 4:12

Therefore thus I will do to you, O Israel;
 because I will do this to you, prepare to
 meet your God, O Israel!

Amos 4:12

God is passionately interested in his people. He will not acquiesce in their continuous indifference. He will not take no for an answer. He will not busy himself in some other part of the universe and leave them alone. There will be a meeting!

How do you prepare to meet God?

PRAYER: "O Jesus, Thou art standing Outside the fast-closed door, In lowly patience waiting To pass the threshold o'er: Shame on us, Christian brothers, His name and sign who bear, O shame, thrice shame upon us, To keep Him standing there!" (William Walsham How, "O Jesus, Thou Art Standing," *The Hymnbook*, 266). *Amen.*

"The Lord, the God of Hosts"

Read Amos 4:13

For lo, the one who forms the mountains,
   creates the wind, reveals his thoughts to
   mortals, makes the morning darkness,
   and treads on the heights of the earth—
   the Lord, the God of hosts, is his name!

Amos 4:13

There is no trifling with the God who shattered Gomorrah and shaped Sinai. He will not be exiled to the backwoods of our existence; he will not be reduced to the role of absentee landlord. There is no avoiding his presence; there is no escaping his action; there is no defense against his will.

How does God penetrate your defenses?

PRAYER: "O Jesus, Thou art pleading In accents meek and low, 'I died for you, My children, And will ye treat Me so?' O Lord, with shame and sorrow We open now the door; Dear Saviour, enter, enter, And leave us nevermore!" (William Walsham How, "O Jesus, Thou Art Standing," *The Hymnbook*, 266). Amen.

"In Lamentation"

Read Amos 5:1–3

Hear this word that I take up over you
   in lamentation, O house of Israel:
Fallen, no more to rise, is maiden
Israel; forsaken on her land, with
no one to raise her up.

Amos 5:1–2

The lamentation was a poem expressing grief over a friend's death. Amos sings it over the corpse of his people. The effect would be something like the "shock of reading one's own obituary in the newspaper" (James Mays).

Compare this with Lamentations 1:1.

PRAYER: God, you take my life so much more seriously than I take it. You have such magnificent plans for me, and I respond by wasting time and talents, squandering grace, and trivializing love. Forgive me and restore me to a life of glad and noble seriousness. *Amen.*

"Do Not Seek Bethel"

Read Amos 5:4–5

But do not seek Bethel, and do not enter
into Gilgal or cross over to Beer-sheba;
for Gilgal shall surely go into exile,
and Bethel shall come to nothing.

Amos 5:5

A place of worship ought to be a place where mind and spirit are directed to God's will, a place of concentration and purification. In Israel, it was not so: worship was a distraction from God, a diversion from his ways.

What is your place of worship like?

PRAYER: Lord Jesus Christ, guard me from religious nonsense and pious playacting. When I worship, let me be heart and soul concerned with you alone and your will in my life. *Amen.*

NOVEMBER 1

"Seek the Lord and Live"
Read Amos 5:6–7

Seek the Lord and live, or he will break out
  against the house of Joseph like fire, and
  it will devour Bethel, with no one to
  quench it.

Amos 5:6

The living, personal God who created life continues to be its source. There is no life apart from
him. If for no other reason than self-preservation,
our lives need to be centered on him.

What does "justice to wormwood" mean?

PRAYER: I will seek you, Lord: I will order the
hours of this day under your command; I will
enter this day's routines in your love; I will perform this day's duties by your grace; in and
through the power of Jesus Christ. *Amen.*

"Who Made the Pleiades"

Read Amos 5:8–9

The one who made the Pleiades and Orion,
and turns deep darkness into the morning, and darkens the day into night, who
calls for the waters of the sea, and pours
them out on the surface of the earth, the
Lord is his name.

Amos 5:8

Amos's task is to get the people to connect what they know of the God of cosmic creation, who no one doubts is majestic and powerful, with the God of personal justice, who is concerned with every detail of morality and love expressed in our daily lives.

Compare this with Psalm 19.

PRAYER: When I look at the skies, O God, there is no doubt in my mind of your power and your glory; it is harder to believe that you are, in the same powerful and glorious way, concerned with my everyday actions. Help me to respond to your revelation inwardly in the same way that I do out-wardly, and so live by your will and to your glory. *Amen.*

"It Is an Evil Time"

Read Amos 5:10–13

Therefore the prudent will keep silent
in such a time; for it is an evil time.

Amos 5:13

Amos evaluates a culture, not in terms of its beauty or its wealth or its success, but by the way it treats the poor, is concerned with justice, and shares compassion.

Is our time better or worse than the time of Amos?

PRAYER: God of compassion and justice, help me to see through what human beings think is important into what you have determined to be essential—matters of the heart, the concerns of conscience, the sufferings of the poor; in Jesus' name. *Amen.*

"Seek Good and Not Evil"
Read Amos 5:14–15

Seek good and not evil, that you may live;
and so the Lord, the God of hosts, will
be with you, just as you have said.

Amos 5:14

Our lives are not manufactured by our culture—
we choose between good and evil. The choices
become our acts, the acts become our habits, and
the habits become our character.

What choices have you made recently to seek
good?

PRAYER: "Listen, Yahweh, I'm calling at the top of
my lungs: 'Be good to me! Answer me!' When my
heart whispered, 'Seek God,' my whole being
replied, 'I'm seeking him!' Don't hide from me
now!" (Psalm 27:7–9). Amen.

"Alas for You"

Read Amos 5:16–20

Alas for you who desire the day of the
Lord! Why do you want the day of
the Lord! It is darkness, not light.

Amos 5:18

The people talked of wanting God at the same time
that they rejected the word of the man of God,
Amos. They wanted to deal directly with God, not
with this rude prophet. Well, they would deal with
him all right—and find some surprises.

Why is Amos's message still necessary?

PRAYER: God, deepen my comprehension of your
ways among this people and enlarge my understanding of your will in my life, so that I may treat
no person with triviality nor live a single hour
gracelessly. *Amen.*

"Let Justice Roll Down"

Read Amos 5:21–28

But let justice roll down like waters, and
    righteousness like an ever-flowing
    stream.

Amos 5:24

If worship does not lead to the protection of the
weak and poor (justice) and to whole relationships with others (righteousness), God hates it.
Worship that does not flow into the community
in streams of justice and righteousness stagnates
and stinks.

What are the consequences of your worship?

PRAYER: God of justice and righteousness, take
every hymn I sing to you, every offering I make to
you, every act of worship I direct to you and
shape them into just acts and righteous relationships so that I may continue your works in the
world, in and through Jesus Christ. *Amen.*

NOVEMBER 7

"At Ease in Zion"

Read Amos 6:1–3

Alas for those who are at ease in Zion, and
for those who feel secure on Mount
Samaria, the notables of the first of the
nations, to whom the house of Israel
resorts!

Amos 6:1

The purpose of the gospel is not to make us comfortable at any cost, but to put us right with God and our neighbor at a cost of nothing less than everything. Christ did not die for us to give us a higher standard of living, but to save us from our sins.

PRAYER: God of all peace, when I hastily take shortcuts to your presence, show me my error. When I thoughtlessly substitute being comfortable for being obedient, expose my sloth. In Jesus' name. *Amen.*

"Beds of Ivory"

Read Amos 6:4–7

Alas for those who lie on beds of ivory, and
    lounge on their couches, and eat lambs
    from the flock, and calves from the stall.
Amos 6:4

Elaborate comforts that divert us from being with
people who suffer, and useless luxuries that keep
us from sharing the basic needs of those around
us, are an affront to the conscience and a scandal
to righteousness.

What comforts keep you from being attentive
to others?

PRAYER: Righteous Lord, break through the barri-
ers that my standard of living puts up between me
and the poor, and establish me in a relationship of
love and justice with them, for Jesus' sake. *Amen.*

"I Abhor the Pride of Jacob"

Read Amos 6:8

The Lord God has sworn by himself (says
the Lord, the God of hosts): I abhor the
pride of Jacob and hate his strongholds;
and I will deliver up the city and all that
is in it.

Amos 6:8

The very thing that gets us promotions in our
work and fame in our society is exposed by the
prophet as the basic sin, pride. It seduces us into
supposing that we can dispense with God and run
our own lives. But we can't.

What are the signs of pride in our society?

PRAYER: "Lord Jesus, I long to be perfectly whole;
I want You forever to live in my soul, break down
every idol, cast out every foe; Now wash me and
I shall be whiter than snow" (J. L. Nicholson,
"Whiter Than Snow," Inspiring Hymns, 382). Amen.

"Shattered to Bits"

Read Amos 6:9–11

> See, the Lord commands, and the great
>   house shall be shattered to bits, and the
>   little house to pieces.
>
> *Amos 6:11*

These terse, enigmatic pieces of conversation and oracle are clear in this: when the judgment of God empties Israel of pride, there will be nothing left to boast about—not population, not buildings, not even religion.

Who in our society is most liable to judgment?

PRAYER: Great God of grace, show me the needs of the people around me, and then give me the courage to work with and on behalf of those who are too weak to help themselves. *Amen.*

NOVEMBER 11

"Plow the Sea with Oxen"
Read Amos 6:12–14

Do horses run on rocks? Does one plow
the sea with oxen? But you have turned
justice into poison and the fruit of
righteousness into wormwood.

Amos 6:12

Israel was attempting the impossible—to be a nation without honoring or obeying God. As well try to run a horse race down a rocky crag, or plow a field in the middle of the ocean. But such absurdities were so commonplace among this people that they no longer even attracted attention.

Does our society engage in similar absurdities?

PRAYER: Dear God, fasten my attention on the clear word that you have given me in scripture, so that I may order my life with the common sense of righteousness and treat others with the plain logic of justice. *Amen.*

NOVEMBER 12

"Locusts"

Read Amos 7:1–3

This is what the Lord God showed me:
  he was forming locusts at the time
  the latter growth began to sprout (it
  was the latter growth after the king's
  mowings).

Amos 7:1

Prophetic intercession spares the people a devastating judgment. Amos makes no excuses for his people; he provides no defense for his nation; he prays knowing that forgiveness alone can change the consequences of the people's sin.

Compare this act of intercession with that of Moses in Numbers 14:11ff.

PRAYER: God, I know that only by means of Christ my intercessor can I stand before you, forgiven and free. I thank you for your deep mercy and powerful love. *Amen.*

"Fire"

This is what the Lord God showed me:
  the Lord God was calling for a shower
of fire, and it devoured the great deep
and was eating up the land.

Amos 7:4

The form of this intercession is nearly identical to that in the previous vision (7:1–3), except that the means of judgment is fire instead of locusts. The repetition emphasizes the readiness of God to respond to the prayer of intercession.

For whom do you pray in intercession?

PRAYER: Lord, these are the people whom I know to be in deep need, suffering the consequences of sin, caught in the meshes of suffering. Be with them in forgiving love, in sustaining comfort, in saving peace. *Amen.*

"A Plumb Line"

Read Amos 7:7–9

> And the Lord said to me, "Amos, what do
> you see?" And I said, "A plumb line."
> Then the Lord said, "See, I am setting a
> plumb line in the midst of my people
> Israel; I will never again pass them by."
>
> Amos 7:8

The plumb line is a standard against which we measure whether our walls are built correctly: are they upright or askew? vertical to the base or crazily aslant? In the same way that gravity holds a plumb line to everything built on earth, so grace holds it to everything built toward heaven.

What is the plumb line with which God tests your life?

PRAYER: Not only, Lord, do you give solid foundations to my life, you provide accurate directions for my growth. Using the standards of your word, I want to grow up "to the measure of the full stature of Christ" (Ephesians 4:13b). Amen.

"*Amaziah*"

Read Amos 7:10–13

Then Amaziah, the priest of Bethel, sent to
King Jeroboam of Israel, saying, "Amos
has conspired against you in the very
center of the house of Israel; the land is
not able to bear all his words."

Amos 7:10

The conflict between Amaziah and Amos is the
classic conflict between religious words put in the
service of human beings to justify and comfort
them, and religious commitment put in the service of God to declare his will and represent his
ways.

Do you know any religious leaders like Amaziah?

PRAYER: God, keep me open to all courageous
prophets and wary of all sycophantic priests. Help
me to tell the difference between the words men
and women use to make me feel good and those
you use to make me good, in Jesus Christ. *Amen.*

"A Dresser of Sycamore Trees"

Read Amos 7:14–15

> Then Amos answered Amaziah, "I am no
> prophet, nor a prophet's son; but I am
> a herdsman, and a dresser of sycamore
> trees."

Amos 7:14

Amos has no profession to defend, no special priv-
ileges to protect: he has humble origins and unim-
pressive credentials. His only reason for speaking
is that God has spoken; his only qualification for
being a prophet, God's call.

What did Amaziah think of Amos?

PRAYER: "God of the prophets! Bless the prophets'
sons; Elijah's mantle o'er Elisha cast; Each age its
solemn task may claim but once; Make each one
nobler, stronger than the last" (Denis Wortman,
"God of the Prophets," *The Hymnbook*, 520). *Amen*

"Exile"

Read Amos 7:16–17

Therefore thus says the Lord: "Your wife
shall become a prostitute in the city, and
your sons and your daughters shall fall
by the sword, and your land shall be
parceled out by line; you yourself shall
die in an unclean land, and Israel shall
surely go into exile away from its land."

Amos 7:17

Amaziah attempted to silence not Amos but God.
He was more concerned with protecting the king
from irritation than with saving the people from
judgment. Amos's vehement response has all the
passion of violated holiness.

What was the issue between Amos and Amaziah?

PRAYER: Righteous Father, your justice is an immense glory; help me never to shrug it off as an
inconvenience. Your judgments are awesome realities; help me never to trivialize them into items
of etiquette. For Jesus' sake. *Amen.*

"A Basket of Summer Fruit"

Read *Amos* 8:1–3

This is what the Lord God showed me—a
basket of summer fruit.

Amos 8:1

The significance of this vision involves a play on
words: the word for "summer fruit" is *qayits*; the
word for "end" is *qets*. The vision is a reminder of
a deadline: the end is at hand. There is no more
time for procrastination.

Do you work better with a deadline?

PRAYER: I remember your clear words, Lord, "The
kingdom of God is at hand; repent and believe in
the Gospel" (Mark 1:15), and I know that I cannot saunter through faith, window-shopping for
grace. Thank you for the reminder. *Amen.*

"Buying the Poor for Silver"

Read Amos 8:4–6

> Saying, "When will the new moon be
> over so that we may sell grain; and the
> sabbath, so that we may offer wheat for
> sale? We will make the ephah small and
> the shekel great, and practice deceit with
> false balances, buying the poor for silver
> and the needy for a pair of sandals, and
> selling the sweepings of the wheat."
>
> *Amos 8:5–6*

Amos was preaching in a society that put far more value on possessions than on people. The price of a poor person was approximately that of a pair of sandals. When values have become that twisted, the judgment of God is bound to be severe.

Do you ever "put a price" on people?

PRAYER: God, I know that every person I meet was "bought with a price" (1 Corinthians 6:20), and must not be treated cheaply by me. As I learn my own worth and dignity in Jesus Christ, help me to see others in the same way. *Amen.*

"Like the Nile of Egypt"

Read Amos 8:7–8

Shall not the land tremble on this account,
    and everyone mourn who lives in it, and
    all of it rise like the Nile, and be tossed
    about and sink again, like the Nile of
    Egypt?

Amos 8:8

The uncontrollable floodwaters of the Nile, which rose and fell seasonally, are a picture of what will happen when God's judgments sweep down upon people living complacently in fraudulently acquired security.

How is a flood a good image for judgment?

PRAYER: Dear Lord, show me how to build my life on the rock foundations of your word, so that when the rains fall and the floods rise I may stand "steadfast, unmovable, always abounding in the work of the Lord" (1 Corinthians 15:58). *Amen.*

NOVEMBER 21

"A Bitter Day"

Read Amos 8:9–10

I will turn your feasts into mourning,
    and all your songs into lamentation;
    I will bring sackcloth on all loins, and
    baldness on every head; I will make it
    like the mourning for an only son, and
    the end of it like a bitter day.

Amos 8:10

The prophetic word hammers away, relentlessly trying to penetrate the thick defenses of excuse-making and rationalization. Amos uses every picture he can paint, every memory he can revive, every terror he can imagine in order to warn the people and get them to repent.

How many illustrations are in this passage?

PRAYER: Father in heaven, if I have blind spots in my vision, cure them so that I may see the sins that hurt others and grieve you. I don't want the judgment to come upon me unawares, but would live each day in the light of your word in Jesus Christ. *Amen.*

"I Will Send a Famine"

Read *Amos* 8:11–12

The time is surely coming, says the Lord
God, when I will send a famine on the
land; not a famine of bread, or a thirst
for water, but of hearing the words of
the Lord.

Amos 8:11–12

It was laid down by Moses and repeated by Jesus,
"Man shall not live by bread alone, but by every
word that proceeds from the mouth of God"
(Deuteronomy 8:3; Matthew 4:4). If people are
deprived of the divine word, their spirits will become as gaunt and desperate as the victims of any
famine.

How do you show your appreciation for God's
word?

PRAYER: "How I love Thy law, O Lord! Daily joy its
truths afford; in its constant light I go, wise to con-
quer every foe. Sweeter are Thy words to me than
all other good can be; safe I walk, Thy truth my
light, hating falsehood, loving right" (*The Psalter*,
1912). *Amen.*

"They Shall Fall"

Read Amos 8:13–14

Those who swear by Ashimah of Samaria,
    and say, "As your god lives, O Dan,"
    and, "As the way of Beer-sheba lives"—
they shall fall, and never rise again.

Amos 8:14

Those who persist in ignoring or denying God will get what they have asked for: his absence. And then no amount of searching, even though a person may travel from Dan in the north to Beer-sheba in the south, will find him.

Do you know where Dan and Beer-sheba are located?

PRAYER: I thank you, Lord, for your presence, "nearer than breathing, closer than hands or feet" (*The Book of Common Worship*, 330). I will diligently enter into your will this day and "practice the presence" happily, for Jesus' sake and by his grace. Amen.

"Strike the Capitals"

Read Amos 9:1

I saw the Lord standing beside the altar,
and he said: Strike the capitals until the
thresholds shake, and shatter them on
the heads of the people; and those who
are left I will kill with the sword; not
one of them shall flee away, not one of
them shall escape.

Amos 9:1

The surprise in this vision is its location, "beside the altar." The people had mistakenly thought that if they showed they were on God's side by frequenting the sacred places, God would be on their side. He will be there all right, but in judgment.

Compare this with 1 Peter 4:17.

PRAYER: "Judge eternal, throned in splendor, Lord of Lords and King of Kings, With Thy living fire of judgment Purge our land of bitter things: Solace all its wide dominion With the healing of Thy wings" (Henry Scott Holland, "Judge Eternal, Throned in Splendor," *The Hymnbook*, 517). Amen.

NOVEMBER 25

"Though They Dig into Sheol"
Read Amos 9:2–4

Though they dig into Sheol, from there
  shall my hand take them; though they
  climb up to heaven, from there I will
  bring them down.

Amos 9:2

No hole is deep enough, no mountain high
enough, and no trip long enough to escape God's
presence. He will get to us. The question is not,
Will we be with God? but, Will we unsuccessfully
run from his judgment or confidently embrace
his salvation?

Compare this with Psalm 139:7–12.

PRAYER: Thank you, Father, for not leaving me
alone when I leave you, for not ignoring me
when I hide from you. Always, you have sought
me. Ever do you find me. Glory be to your name.
Amen.

"The Lord, God of Hosts"

Read Amos 9:5–6

The Lord, God of hosts, he who touches
the earth and it melts, and all who live
in it mourn, and all of it rises like the
Nile, and sinks again, like the Nile of
Egypt.

Amos 9:5

One reason people continue in sin is that they
think of God as a kind of holy relic that can be
stored in the attic and taken out to play with on
rainy days. If ever they once realized his cosmic
majesty and towering will, they might leave off
their paltry ways and stunted values, repent, and
live on the scale for which they were created.

Is your idea of God too small?

PRAYER: "Your thoughts—how rare, how beautiful! God, I'll never comprehend them! . . . Investigate my life, O God, find out everything about
me; cross-examine and test me, get a clear picture of what I'm about; see for yourself whether
I've done anything wrong—then guide me on
the road to eternal life." (Psalm 139:17, 23–24).
Amen.

"Not Utterly Destroy"
Read Amos 9:7–8

The eyes of the Lord God are upon the
  sinful kingdom, and I will destroy it
  from the face of the earth—except that
  I will not utterly destroy the house of
  Jacob, says the Lord.

Amos 9:8

However severe the announced judgment, however sweeping the prophetic indictment, however
unsparing the angry sermons, the end is not destruction. God's word is not designed to consign
everyone to despair but to arouse all to repentance.

What is the single most helpful word in this
passage?

PRAYER: Lord God, help me to take seriously every
word of judgment that you pronounce without
ever feeling that you have given up on me, but
with an awakened confidence that you will save
and redeem me, even in Jesus Christ. Amen.

"As One Shakes with a Sieve"
Read Amos 9:9–10

For lo, I will command, and shake the
house of Israel among all the nations as
one shakes with a sieve, but no pebble
shall fall to the ground.

Amos 9:9

Amos, as is his custom, uses experiences out of
his own rural, agricultural life to make God's word
plain. The sieve was a large mesh for separating
grain from any stones or other foreign matter that
the winnowing process had not already elimi-
nated. The point is that "successful" sinners would
not get by forever unscathed by judgment.

Are there people who you think have "gotten
away with" evil?

PRAYER: "Just as I am, without one plea But that
Thy blood was shed for me, And that Thou bid-
dest me come to Thee, O Lamb of God, I come, I
come!" (Charlotte Elliott, "Just as I Am, Without
One Plea," *The Hymnbook*, 272). *Amen.*

"I Will Raise Up"

Read Amos 9:11–12

On that day I will raise up the booth
of David that is fallen, and repair its
breaches, and raise up its ruins, and
rebuild it as in the days of old.

Amos 9:11

Amos's theme throughout has been the doom of
judgment; the final note is a gloriously happy
restoration. The time of David was, in retrospect,
the golden age—a time of national security and of
spiritual vitality. What was, will be again.

What is meant by "the booth of David"?

PRAYER: Come, Lord Jesus, and from the rubble of
my confessed sins and lamented wrongs build a
temple for your Holy Spirit, so that my life may be
evidence of your salvation and a witness to your
grace. Amen.

"The Mountains Shall Drip Sweet Wine"
Read Amos 9:13–15

The time is surely coming, says the Lord,
    when the one who plows shall overtake
    the one who reaps, and the treader of
    grapes the one who sows the seed; the
    mountains shall drip sweet wine, and
    all the hills shall flow with it.

Amos 9:13

If we shut up the Bible whenever we read something unpleasant, turn away when its message is too harsh for our ears, or close its pages too soon, we will not get to the end of the story, which is not doom but salvation.

How would you summarize Amos's "last word"?

PRAYER: God, give me the perseverance to accept whatever judgment you set upon my life, to go through whatever trials you decide are best, unflinchingly accepting the disciplines of your love, and finally experiencing in all its glory your salvation. In Jesus' name. *Amen.*

DECEMBER 1

"Micah of Moresheth"

Read Micah 1:1

The word of the Lord that came to Micah
of Moresheth in the days of Kings
Jotham, Ahaz, and Hezekiah of Judah,
which he saw concerning Samaria and
Jerusalem.

Micah 1:1

Prophets are important because they tell us how
things look from God's point of view. The prophet
Micah was a contemporary of Isaiah and Hosea
(in the eighth century B.C.). His name—which
means "who is like the Lord?"—is also his message: he directs people away from a selfish preoccupation with themselves to obedient faith in a
living God.

What do you know about the eighth century
B.C.?

PRAYER: God, use Micah's message to draw me
away from merely looking after myself and wasting my life in selfish pursuits. Then pull me toward you, the living God of health and salvation.
In Jesus' name. *Amen.*

"The Lord Is Coming Out"
Read Micah 1:2–9

For lo, the Lord is coming out of his place,
and will come down and tread upon the
high places of the earth.

Micah 1:3

Some people had settled into ways that were easy and comfortable for them but left others in great deprivation and pain. They supposed that God was benignly indifferent to what they did, that he was distant and passive. But God is interested and active, and judgment is the proof of it.

What happens when God "comes out"?

PRAYER: X-ray my heart, O God. Show me the moral muscle that has softened into flabby indifference, the spiritual trust that has bloated into presumption. Then, having shown me my heart, cure me with surgical judgment, for Jesus Christ's sake. *Amen.*

"Make Yourselves Bald"

Read Micah 1:10–16

Make yourselves bald and cut off your
  hair for your pampered children; make
  yourselves as bald as the eagle, for they
  have gone from you into exile.

Micah 1:16

Each town is a text. The sound of the town's name
triggers a blast of judgment. Communities that
were intended to be centers for administering justice and sharing love have, instead, earned a reputation for oppression.

How many towns are mentioned?

PRAYER: God, my first impulse on learning that
my sins are found out is to run away and hide. But
there is no place secure from your judgment; help
me to confess my sins and receive your salvation
so that I am ready for your judgment. *Amen.*

"Alas"

Read Micah 2:1–5

Alas for those who devise wickedness
  and evil deeds on their beds! When
  the morning dawns, they perform it,
  because it is in their power.

Micah 2:1

There are people who sin night and day: during
the night, the imagination works out plans to get
the better of others; throughout the day, the cov-
etous plans are put into action. Do the hapless and
weak stand a chance against such total and single-
minded selfishness? Yes, for God will finally put a
stop to it with his "Alas."

What do the two "therefores" conclude?

PRAYER: Father, you have given me the great gift
of imagination; help me to use it in good and
original ways, at night dreaming up new ways
to love, in the day finding fresh opportunities to
help. *Amen.*

"Do Not Preach"

Read Micah 2:6–11

"Do not preach"—thus they preach—
  "one should not preach of such things;
  disgrace will not overtake us."

Micah 2:6

People do not want to hear what Micah has to preach: they prefer a preacher who tells them that everything will turn out all right. Any sanctimonious windbag (see v. 11) who tells the people that they can do anything that makes them feel good, and everything will turn out all right, is preferred to Micah's true and prophetic preaching. The truth hurts.

Why was Micah's message opposed?

PRAYER: O God, I need to hear life-changing truth, not soothing lies. I want your soul-baring sword-words, not frivolous, decorative, "uplifting" thoughts. Address me, in Christ, in the depths of my being, where new life is shaped by your Spirit. Amen.

DECEMBER 6

"I Will Gather"
Read Micah 2:12–13

I will surely gather all of you, O Jacob, I
will gather the survivors of Israel; I will
set them together like sheep in a fold,
like a flock in its pasture; it will resound
with people.

Micah 2:12

A selecting, winnowing process is at work among
God's people. Despite the appearance of widespread indifference in the land, this remnant-
making work is continuously taking place. God
calls together those who will live by faith, who
will walk in obedience, who will work in love.

Who are the survivors of Israel?

PRAYER: Lord Jesus Christ, you are my shepherd,
calling and leading me. With you as my shepherd,
I will be content to be numbered in the little
flock. Keep me responsive to your leadership, to
what you say and how you guide. *Amen.*

"Chop Them Up Like Meat"

Read Micah 3:1–4

You who hate the good and love the evil,
who tear the skin off my people, and the
flesh off their bones; who eat the flesh
of my people, flay their skin off them,
break their bones in pieces, and chop
them up like meat in a kettle, like flesh
in a caldron.

Micah 3:2–3

Instead of ruling the people in justice and love, those in authority were exploiting them—an old story. Micah's language is designed to shock the rulers into an awareness of the ruthless cruelty of their policies.

What will happen to the corrupt rulers?

PRAYER: From your throne, Almighty God, you rule in perfect justice: help me to use whatever authority I have—as a parent, as a worker, as a citizen—to look out for the well-being of those around me and share your love with them. *Amen.*

"The Seers Shall Be Disgraced"
Read Micah 3:5–7

The seers shall be disgraced, and the
diviners put to shame; they shall all
cover their lips, for there is no answer
from God.

Micah 3:7

The prophets had become commercialized: you
got what you paid for. A healthy fee bought a
promise of peace; inability to pay brought down
a curse of enmity.

What will happen to the venal prophets?

PRAYER: "Riches I heed not, nor man's empty
praise, Thou mine inheritance, now and always:
Thou and Thou only, first in my heart, High King
of heaven, my Treasure Thou art" (Ancient Irish
hymn, "Be Thou My Vision," *The Hymnbook*, 303).
Amen.

"But as for Me"

Read Micah 3:8

But as for me, I am filled with power,
   with the spirit of the Lord, and with
   justice and might, to declare to Jacob
   his transgression and to Israel his sin.

Micah 3:8

True prophets go against the stream of popular expectation and refuse to turn religion into either an entertainment or a commodity. No matter how prevalent the general apostasy, there are always some, like Micah, who obediently and faithfully speak God's word.

Whom do you know who is like Micah?

PRAYER: Father, you have created me with a purpose. You have saved me to use me. Clarify your will in me and fill me with your Spirit, so that I may do that which I have been set apart to do, in Jesus Christ. *Amen.*

"Zion Shall Be Plowed"

Read Micah 3:9–12

> Therefore because of you Zion shall be
> plowed as a field; Jerusalem shall
> become a heap of ruins, and the
> mountain of the house a wooded
> height.

Micah 3:12

A ramshackle superstructure of politics and religion had been built on the field set apart for growing the fruits of the Spirit. God's judgment will tear it down and start over. It is back to the basics: plowing the field and planting a new crop of righteousness from which a harvest of praise can be gathered.

Who was responsible for the sin?

PRAYER: I confess, merciful Lord, that very often I have done just the opposite of what you intended—getting instead of giving, boasting instead of praising, pushing others out of my way instead of pulling them into my embrace. Forgive me and start over with me for Jesus' sake. *Amen.*

"Swords into Plowshares"

Read Micah 4:1–4

He shall judge between many peoples, and
   shall arbitrate between strong nations
   far away; they shall beat their swords
   into plowshares, and their spears into
   pruning hooks; nation shall not lift up
   sword against nation, neither shall they
   learn war any more.

Micah 4:3

This powerful and attractive vision catches the attention of all who are tired of war and fed up with selfishness. What God intends for his people matches what we long for—thus the vision shapes present actions in ways of peace.

What do you like about this vision?

PRAYER: "Be Thou my Vision, O Lord of my heart; Nought be all else to me, save that Thou art—Thou my best thought, by day or by night, Waking or sleeping, Thy presence my light" (Ancient Irish hymn, "Be Thou My Vision," *The Hymnbook*, 303). *Amen.*

DECEMBER 12

"We Will Walk"

Read Micah 4:5

For all the peoples walk, each in the
name of its god, but we will walk in
the name of the Lord our God forever
and ever.

Micah 4:5

Belief is the source of behavior. What we think about God shapes what we do in our everyday lives. There is nothing more practical than religion, no more down-to-earth decision to be made than about God.

What difference does your belief make in your behavior?

PRAYER: When I worship you, Holy God, I am not diverted into fantasy but plunged into reality. I find all my actions more sure and all my thoughts more certain. Thank you, in the name of Jesus Christ. Amen.

"I Will Assemble the Lame"

Read Micah 4:6–7

In that day, says the Lord, I will assemble
the lame and gather those who have
been driven away, and those whom
I have afflicted.

Micah 4:6

Our infatuation with power and our adoration of
glamour are not biblical. God takes what we reject
as useless and inadequate ("the low and despised
in the world"—1 Corinthians 1:27–28) to form
the community that will receive and express his
grace.

What does he mean by the lame?

PRAYER: You yourself, Christ, were a rejected stone
but have become the cornerstone of salvation. Take
my inadequacies—my experiences of rejection,
my feelings of inferiority—and use them as raw
materials to construct trust in your wisdom and
faith in your strength. *Amen.*

DECEMBER 14

"O Tower of the Flock"

Read Micah 4:8

And you, O tower of the flock, hill of
daughter Zion, to you it shall come,
the former dominion shall come, the
sovereignty of daughter Jerusalem.

Micah 4:8

The purposed but tarnished hope that God's people
will provide spiritual leadership to the nations will
be cleaned by the scrub brush of judgment and set
gleaming before the people again. As the old Puritan
pastor Thomas Goodwin has it, "All God's
grace is coined out of purposes into promises."

Who is the "tower of the flock"?

PRAYER: God, the bright hopes you once gave me
have been dulled by my faithlessness. Clarify the
memory of your splendid promises to me; restore
the dazzling image of your fullness in me; in and
through Jesus Christ. Amen.

DECEMBER 15

"Writhe and Groan"

Read Micah 4:9–10

Writhe and groan, O daughter Zion, like
a woman in labor; for now you shall
go forth from the city and camp in the
open country; you shall go to Babylon.
There you shall be rescued, there the
Lord will redeem you from the hands
of your enemies.

Micah 4:10

Judgment hurts. But it is pain with a purpose, like
the pains of childbirth. Besides announcing the
judgment, Micah declares the redemption that
will come out of it.

What will happen in Babylon?

PRAYER: God, show me the lines of redemption
that can be traced in every pain and in every disappointment. Prepare my heart with hope to receive the wholeness that you have for me. Lead
me through the testing into the peace of Christ.
Amen.

"Arise and Thresh"

Read Micah 4:11–13

Arise and thresh, O daughter Zion, for
I will make your horn iron and your
hoofs bronze; you shall beat in pieces
many peoples, and shall devote their
gain to the Lord, their wealth to the
Lord of the whole earth.

Micah 4:13

Not only are God's people disciplined through
judgment to holiness, they are also the means of
exercising judgment upon others. The day will
come when both persecuted and persecutors will
be placed before the Lord as an offering.

What does threshing do?

PRAYER: I get fleeting glimpses of your compre-
hensive plan, eternal Lord, and realize that your
will is working in everyone, in every nation, in all
cultures, throughout time and space, and grate-
fully know that "all will be well and all manner of
things will be well" (Julian of Norwich). Amen.

DECEMBER 17

"Siege Is Laid Against Us"
Read Micah 5:1

Now you are walled around with a wall;
  siege is laid against us; with a rod they
  strike the ruler of Israel upon the cheek.
                                              Micah 5:1

This fourth "now" (see chap. 4, vv. 9–11) emphasizes the present difficulties that are a result of corrupt government and faithless religion. A true prophet never avoids dealing with what is wrong but brings it out into the open. Prophets do not fake optimism; they encourage a sense of reality, even when the reality involves humiliation and judgment.

How did things get so bad?

PRAYER: God, in Christ you have entered into what I have to face every day: the shoddy morality of this society, my own weak and fickle will, the wrecked visions of the age. There is not much to hope for in these ruins. I wait for your word, and hope in your salvation. *Amen.*

DECEMBER 18

"O Bethlehem of Ephrathah"

Read Micah 5:2–4

But you, O Bethlehem of Ephrathah, who
are one of the little clans of Judah, from
you shall come forth for me one who is
to rule in Israel, whose origin is from of
old, from ancient days.

Micah 5:2

God will give the people a ruler—a messiah!—
whose authority is independent of an army or
popularity. God's ruler will be everything that
they need; he will be what they have never gotten
from their faithless priests and corrupt rulers.

Read the fulfillment of this prophecy in
Matthew 2:1–6.

PRAYER: "O holy Child of Bethlehem, Descend to
us, we pray; Cast out our sin, and enter in, Be born
in us today. We hear the Christmas angels The great
glad tidings tell; O come to us, abide with us, Our
Lord Emmanuel" (Phillips Brooks, "O Little Town
of Bethlehem," *The Hymnbook*, 171). *Amen.*

DECEMBER 19

"One of Peace"

Read Micah 5:5–9

And he shall be the one of peace. If the
    Assyrians come into our land and tread
    upon our soil, we will raise against them
    seven shepherds and eight installed as
    rulers.

Micah 5:5

Peace is not timidity: it is confrontation with the arrogant marauders (Nimrod!) and a righteous infiltration throughout the peoples of the earth ("like dew from the Lord"). God is on the move to make his people whole, and by means of them, all people.

Where else have you read of the remnant?

PRAYER: Almighty God, as I submit myself to your promises, work your will in me, "that which is pleasing in your sight" (Hebrews 13:21). I give you my anxieties and weakness: use them to make a strong peace. *Amen.*

"Cut Off Your Horses"
Read Micah 5:10–15

In that day, says the Lord, I will cut off
   your horses from among you and will
   destroy your chariots.

Micah 5:10

All the ways in which the people were trying to become important—war, horses, sorceries, idols—
will be destroyed so that God can become important to them. Judgment is housecleaning—getting
rid of dirt and junk—in the house of salvation.

What does God need to eliminate in your life?

PRAYER: I drag all kinds of useless trivia into my
life, Lord—trinkets and charms and formulas—
thinking that I am improving myself. But I only
clutter up my life. Clean it all out so that I may live
simply and directly by faith, in the name of Jesus
Christ. Amen.

DECEMBER 21

"Plead Your Case"

Read Micah 6:1–2

Hear what the Lord says: Rise, plead your case before the mountains, and let the hills hear your voice.

Micah 6:1

The celebrated court case *God vs. The People* is brought to trial. The jury is the mountains and hills. The prophet argues the case for the prosecution. Will the people have an adequate defense? What will the verdict be?

What is God's complaint?

PRAYER: "Approach, my soul, the mercy seat, Where Jesus answers prayer; There humbly fall before His feet, For none can perish there. Thy promise is my only plea, With this I venture nigh; Thou callest burdened souls to Thee, And such, O Lord, am I" (John Newton, "Approach, My Soul, the Mercy Seat," *The Hymnbook*, 386). *Amen.*

DECEMBER 22

"Answer Me!"

Read Micah 6:3–5

"O my people, what have I done to you? In
what have I wearied you? Answer me!"

Micah 6:3

The prosecution builds its case on a record of salvation. It becomes obvious that God has done
nothing worthy of rejection and has insisted on
nothing that was burdensome. All his ways have
been deliverance and providence. Let the people
now describe what they have done.

What did Balak do?

PRAYER: Lord, I am forever calling you to account
for what I suppose you are doing or permitting,
always asking for explanations. But you are calling
me to account! Help me to be honest in my confession and courageous in my response. *Amen.*

"What Does the Lord Require?"

Read Micah 6:6–8

He has told you, O mortal, what is good;
 and what does the Lord require of you
 but to do justice, and to love kindness,
 and to walk humbly with your God?

Micah 6:8

The passage is deservedly famous: it contrasts exterior religious window-dressing with interior personal faith; it cuts through the jungle growth of what we do to impress God and makes a plain path out of the simplicities of being honest, responsive, and obedient before God.

How many questions are asked here?

PRAYER: God, you have shown me what is good, and I thank you: now I need your help to stick with it. Grant that this day I will do justice and love kindness and walk humbly before you, in Jesus' name. *Amen.*

"A Gnawing Hunger"
Read Micah 6:9–16

You shall eat, but not be satisfied, and there
    shall be a gnawing hunger within you;
    you shall put away, but not save, and
    what you save, I will hand over to the
    sword.

Micah 6:14

Sin will not satisfy us. Pride will not make us important; riches will not fulfill us; violence will not provide strength. The wholeness that we crave is not given otherwise than by faith.

What are the statutes of Omri?

PRAYER: "My spirit longs for Thee Within my troubled breast, Though I unworthy be Of so divine a Guest. Unworthy though I be, Yet has my heart no rest, Unless it come from Thee" (John Byrom, "My Spirit Longs for Thee," *The Hymnbook*, 321). *Amen.*

"The Faithful Have Disappeared"
Read Micah 7:1–7

The faithful have disappeared from the
land, and there is no one left who is
upright; they all lie in wait for blood,
and they hunt each other with nets.

Micah 7:2

There are times when the cause of God seems hopeless. Elijah had a similar time of discouragement when he felt that he was the only one in Israel who had faith. But his feelings were wrong, for there were yet seven thousand who had not bowed to Baal (1 Kings 19).

How many illustrations are given for the despair?

PRAYER: My hope is not in men and women but in you, O God. When I am disappointed in those around me and disillusioned in those I had supposed would be valiant in faith, let not my despair turn to cynicism; instead, let it inspire fresh devotion to you, in Jesus Christ. *Amen.*

"Then My Enemy Will See"
Read Micah 7:8–10

Then my enemy will see, and shame will
cover her who said to me, "Where is the
Lord your God?" My eyes will see her
downfall; now she will be trodden down
like the mire of the streets.

Micah 7:10

Faith is tuned to a frequency inaudible to doubt. It
is not strange, then, that believers meet with deri-
sion and taunts. "Those who are deaf always despise those who dance" (Alexander Whyte). The
skeptics and the mockers will be routed, though,
for faith triumphs, always.

What will the enemy see?

PRAYER: Lord, sustain me through times when I
see dimly or not at all. Hold me fast in the hours
when I feel emptiness and despair. Stop my ears to
the taunts of doubt, of skepticism, of contempt.
Open my ears to the hallelujah chorus of faith.
Amen.

DECEMBER 27

"Far Extended"

Read Micah 7:11–13

A day for the building of your walls!
In that day the boundary shall be far
extended.

Micah 7:11

Hope shapes the last words. The people of faith
are the agents by which God makes a new city and
blesses a vast land. Wall building and boundary
extension are metaphors of gospel hope.

How far does God's blessing reach?

PRAYER: That which my sin has destroyed, build
up by your grace, O God. That which my rebellion has ruined, remake in salvation. Put me in
your new city of righteousness, where there is
room to obey and love and praise. *Amen.*

"Shepherd Your People"
Read Micah 7:14

Shepherd your people with your staff, the
flock that belongs to you, which lives
alone in a forest in the midst of a garden
land; let them feed in Bashan and Gilead
as in the days of old.

Micah 7:14

The forest, while nice for scenery, is poor for graz-
ing. There is "garden land" on all sides, but an un-
shepherded flock lost in the forest cannot find it.
We need God's guiding hand to lead us out of the
woods into the green pastures.

Compare this with Psalm 23.

PRAYER: Shepherd Lord, my desires lead me off to
places where there is nothing to sustain my spirit,
nothing to nurture either love or righteousness.
Lead me today into the Bashan and Gilead of scripture and prayer, in Jesus' name. *Amen.*

DECEMBER 29

"Marvelous Things"

Read Micah 7:15

As in the days when you came out of
the land of Egypt, show us marvelous
things.

Micah 7:15

The Exodus deliverance, an unquestioned fact of
history, is proof that God acts to save: what God
did, he does, and will do. All God's promises are
built upon solid facts of revelation; they are never
spun out of a dream imagination.

What has God yet to do in your life?

PRAYER: Father, sharpen my memory so that I will
know the way you have worked and the things
you have done. Then use these facts to feed my
hope in your promise and my faith in your victory. *Amen.*

DECEMBER 30

"Lick Dust"

Read Micah 7:16–17

They shall lick dust like a snake, like the
crawling things of the earth; they shall
come trembling out of their fortresses;
they shall turn in dread to the Lord our
God, and they shall stand in fear of you.

Micah 7:17

When the mountain caves from which we have
waged guerrilla warfare against God are finally
found out, and we come out into the open in fear
and trembling, we will find ourselves in the presence of a God who "does not retain his anger forever, because he delights in showing clemency"
(7:18).

To whom do the words of judgment apply?

PRAYER: God, prepare your way of salvation
through the country of my heart: level the mountains of pride, fill in the swamps of despair, destroy all sin's hideouts, and lead me into faith and
praise. *Amen.*

"Who Is a God Like You?"
Read Micah 7:18–20

Who is a God like you, pardoning iniquity
and passing over the transgression of the
remnant of your possession? He does
not retain his anger forever, because he
delights in showing clemency.

Micah 7:18

The exclamatory question echoes the prophet's
name (*Micah* means "who is like the Lord"). The
quality in God that stands out above all others is
forgiveness—his unwavering willingness to get
rid of our sin and establish us in his love.

How many words for sin are used?

PRAYER: My sins, Lord, in the depths of the sea.
Buried and beyond recovering! What a gospel.
What a Savior. What a God. All praise to Father,
Son, and Spirit. *Amen.*

Topic Index

Scripture Index

7:16 Aug. 29	13:15 Sept. 29
8:1 Aug. 30	14:3 Sept. 30
8:6 Aug. 31	14:4 Oct. 1
8:7 Sept. 1	14:9 Oct. 2
8:11 Sept. 2	
9:1 Sept. 3	AMOS
9:4 Sept. 4	1:1 Oct. 3
9:6 Sept. 5	1:2 Oct. 4
9:7 Sept. 6	1:3 Oct. 5
9:10 Sept. 7	1:6 Oct. 6
9:15 Sept. 8	1:9 Oct. 7
10:2 Sept. 9	1:11 Oct. 8
10:4 Sept. 10	1:13 Oct. 9
10:5 Sept. 11	2:1 Oct. 10
10:8 Sept. 12	2:4 Oct. 11
10:9 Sept. 13	2:6 Oct. 12
10:12 Sept. 14	2:10 Oct, 13
10:14 Sept. 15	2:11 Oct. 14
11:1 Sept. 16	2:14 Oct. 15
11:4 Sept. 17	3:2 Oct. 16
11:7 Sept. 18	3:8 Oct. 17
11:9 Sept. 19	3:9 Oct. 18
11:10 Sept. 20	3:10 Oct. 19
12:1 Sept. 21	3:12 Oct. 20
12:6 Sept. 22	3:15 Oct. 21
12:7 Sept. 23	4:1 Oct. 22
12:13 Sept. 24	4:2 Oct. 23
13:2 Sept. 25	4:4 Oct. 24
13:8 Sept. 26	4:6 Oct. 25
13:13 Sept. 27	4:9 Oct. 26
13:14 Sept. 28	4:11 Oct. 27